Mastering the SPL Library

by Joshua Thijssen

 a php[architect] guide

Mastering the SPL Library - a php[architect] guide

First Edition: July 2013 (Version 1.1)

ISBN: **978-1-940111-00-1**

Produced & Printed in the United States

Disclaimer

Although every effort has been made in the preparation of this book to ensure the accuracy of the information contained therein, this book is provided "as-is" and the publisher, the author(s), their distributors and retailers, as well as all affiliated, related or subsidiary parties take no responsibility for any inaccuracy and any and all damages caused, either directly or indirectly, by the use of such information. We have endeavored to properly provide trademark information on all companies and products mentioned in the book by the appropriate use of capitals. However, we cannot guarantee the accuracy of such information.

musketeers.me, The musketeers.me logo, php[architect], the php[architect] logo, NanoBook and the NanoBook logo are trademarks or registered trademarks of musketeers.me, LLC, its assigns, partners, predecessors and successors.

Written by   Joshua Thijssen

Published by   musketeers.me, LLC.
201 Adams Ave.
Alexandria, VA 22301
USA
240-348-5PHP (240-348-5747)
info@phparch.com / phparch.com

Editor-in-Chief   Beth Tucker Long
Managing Editor   Eli White
Technical Reviewer   Chris Tankersley
Copy Editor   Lori Ann Pannier

Layout and Design   Kevin Bruce

Joshua Thijssen is a freelance consultant, trainer and developer. His passion lies in high-end and complex internet systems, code optimization and server administration. His programming skills include-but are not limited to-PHP, C, Java, and Python, and he has experience on a wide range of operating systems. He is a regular speaker at international conferences and speaks about a wide variety of subjects. You can find his blog on http://www.adayinthelifeof.nl.

Table of Contents

Joshua Thijssen

Joshua Thijssen

Preface

About the Author

The first experience I had with a computer was with the Commodore 64 my dad bought around the time I was five or six years old. Even though playing games on it was just awesome by itself, the thing that really fascinated me was a big matrix poster that my dad created of (probably not all, but a lot of) the C64's memory addresses and their purposes: The places where you could "peek" and "poke." You see, the Internet wasn't as big as it is now, so a lot of time was spent on finding and writing documentation on how to program stuff. That poster by itself was so mesmerizing and complex that I wanted to understand what all those numbers were for and how to use them. At that time I was already playing with BASIC but this made me dive into the 6510 assembly with the help of my dad. Not the first or easiest language that most people nowadays will start with.

A little bit later on, when I held a job as a C-programmer in 1998 or so, a co-worker showed me a "voting" application he had written for the intranet of the company we worked for. We had some new features and ideas we wanted him to add, and just in a matter of minutes he added most of those features. I was stunned: how could somebody adapt such a (presumably) C-based CGI-application so quickly? It turns out that the application was not written in C, but in PHP.

That actually was my first encounter with PHP, which I loved right from the start: getting the job done in a language that was easier than Perl and quicker to program than C. Since then, most of my (online) applications have been written in PHP, while other languages like Python and Java were added to my repertoire later on, but mainly for other purposes. As of today, PHP is my number one language when it comes to online applications.

The SPL is again, one of those things that actually stunned me the first time I encountered it. When I discovered the real power of its iterators and interfaces, I fell in love with it just like I did on first seeing PHP. Hopefully, after reading this book, you will experience the same awesomeness I've encountered the first time using SPL.

Acknowledgements

There are lots of people without whom I would never have been able to write this book. First of all, the loves of my life: Esther and Esmée. Furthermore, the whole PHP community: a very strong community with friends all over the world who not only know everything there is to know about PHP, but also are able to have conversations about other things as well!

I would like to thank the PHPBenelux and the PFZ community, who helped solve some problems and contradictions that I encountered when writing the book. Say hi to them on the Freenode IRC channels #php_bnl and #pfz. And personally, the people who helped me with some specific problems: Stephan Hochdörfer, Stefan Koopmanschap, Jurriën Stutterheim and Etienne Kneuss. Thanks guys!

And last but not least, all the core developers, contributors, testers AND users (that means you too!), of PHP, who all chipped in to make PHP what it is today.

Chapter 1

The SPL Structure

The SPL is a large set of functionality that enriches PHP just like frameworks, extensions or third party classes do. Its functionality is split up into a few major components:

- Data structures
- Iterators
- Interfaces
- Exceptions
- Autoloading
- Miscellaneous functionality

This book will try to explain these components one by one, but sometimes we need to step outside one component and into another one in order to understand it better. When needed, I will refer to other components.

Data Structures

The most unfamiliar component for PHP developers will be the SPL data structures. Everything you can do with these structures you can also do with "normal" arrays, so why do we even need to define additional structures? During this chapter we will elaborate why data structures are important and what the pros and cons are compared to normal PHP arrays.

Iterators

Iterators are a common concept in other languages. Even though the iterators in PHP aren't quite the same, they are still very powerful once you get the hang of them. In this chapter we will explore what iterators are, how they function and what the SPL has to offer.

Interfaces

What is a good template library without interfaces? That is why the SPL has defined a small set of interfaces that can be used for all kinds of purposes. Some of these interfaces are just generic interfaces that serve no additional purpose, while others actually give additional "power" to your objects by hooking directly into the PHP core.

Exceptions

An exception is an exception is an exception. If you have dealt before with frameworks or applications that throw a lot of exceptions, you will know that the statement is certainly not true. Dealing with correctly throwing and catching exceptions will result in a more robust application and better fault handling. The SPL defines a lot of exceptions, each for their own purpose. In this chapter we will show you what kind of exceptions there are and show you in detail what those exceptions are for.

Miscellaneous Functionality

Of course, there are things inside the SPL that don't fall into one of
the above categories. In this chapter we will discuss this functionality.
Most importantly, we will discuss the SPL autoloading, ArrayObject and
FileHandling objects.

The SPL Structure

Chapter
2

Introduction to SPL Data Structures

There is something strange with the SPL data structures: there is nothing you can do with these structures that you cannot do otherwise with standard PHP functionality. And truth be told: most of the time you don't even need to deal with these data structures. However, they do have their advantages so knowing their powers can result in faster code or using less memory, especially when you really need it.

This chapter gives you an introduction to what data structures are, how to "measure" its performance and I will show you what data structures the SPL defines.

On Data Structures

So what actually is a data structure? In essence, a data structure is a particular way of storing and organizing data (we call them elements) inside memory so that it can be used efficiently. Efficiency means they might be fast to retrieve or update or it might be efficient when it comes to memory usage.

My Messy Desk as an Analogy

Let's consider my computer desk. In the age of electronics and paperless offices, I cannot even oversee the amount of papers, books, notes, and other stuff that populates my desk. It can hold a lot of stuff (too much actually), and thus it can be considered as a data structure. However, it's not a very efficient one: if I need to find a book, I have to look under everything else to actually find it. So in a sense: retrieving items is not efficient, let alone actually using the desk.

Now let's consider my wife's desk as another data structure. She always orders her stuff: books by books (alphabetical), papers by the rest of the papers and bills, invoices and all other company stuff is placed neatly into separate drawers. When I need to retrieve something from her desk, I ask politely and within seconds she has found it. Furthermore, her desk looks twice as large as mine even though they are really the same size (I've measured!). She is just so much more efficient in storing stuff.

Now this desk can be considered a much better data structure: fetching information is very quick, and she uses less space than I do but on the other hand: adding more stuff for me is just tossing it onto the big pile, while she has to find the correct spot to place it. So you see every data structure has pros and cons (and so do desks).

Data Structures in PHP

Back to PHP: If you have ever worked with PHP, you are already familiar with one data structure: the array. It contains elements (which by itself can also be an array of course), and you can fetch the elements quite easily by using its index. There is functionality to fetch the data from the array, and there is functionality to manipulate the elements, like sort, shuffle and split functionality etcetera. So you can easily tell it is a data structure.

Another sort-of data structure in PHP is the object. It's a collection of functions and data (methods and properties), and even internally, an object is stored inside a data structure (funny enough, the same structure that is used for PHP arrays). But for now we can consider objects outside of our scope.

Pretty much all other types, like integers, floats and Booleans are so-called scalars. These are variables that can only hold one value at the time.

A string, even though PHP considers them a scalar (is_scalar($str) will return true) can be considered a data structure too. It is a collection that can only store characters though. Unlike arrays, they can only be referenced by a numeric value (the index). But even though you cannot use a string directly as an array, you can fetch and modify their elements just like an array:

```
$s = "hello world";
for ($i=0; $i!=strlen($s); $i++) {
    print $s[$i]  . PHP_EOL;
}
$s[0] = "H";
print $s . PHP_EOL;
```

So strings can be seen as an array of characters but they are stored in a different way. For now we don't consider them as full grown data structures.

As I will show you, most data structures from the outside pretty much work the same way. After all, they are there for you to add, remove, update and maybe sort data. It's the internals of those data structures that differ. Some data structures are very easy, and some of them are very hard, involving lots of math. The reason that some data structures store their elements in a very difficult way is because it might help speed up either retrieval or memory usage on those structures and every structure has its own special usage. For instance, some of them are very useful for retrieving elements very quickly, but they will be slow on inserting those elements, while others might be very quick in both adding and retrieving elements, but use a lot of memory (so you can't add thousands of elements without running out of memory).

Sometimes the differences are very subtle: a data structure can be fast for sequential reads, while it's very slow on random reads. With sequential access we mean that we start looking at the first element, then the second, then the third and so on, just like a `foreach()` loop would do. Random access means we can fetch every element without a particular order. It can start by accessing the first element, the 10th next, then the 25th, then the second and so on.

A more detailed explanation on sequential and random access read will be discussed later on in this book when we talk about (seekable) iterators and interfaces.

So it all boils down to this: you need to use the correct data structure for the correct occasion. They can help you a lot, but they could also hurt performance if not used properly. This chapter will explain the different data structures the SPL has to offer and where and how to use them. In all cases, try benchmarking your application, even with different sets of data to see if changing your data structure really has benefited you.

Big Oh and Big Omega

As I've said before, a data structure is often a compromise between space (memory) and speed. Very fast data structures usually use a lot of memory, while the slower ones are using less memory. But this is not always true: there are some structures that are both fast and don't use a lot of memory, and even the opposite is also possible: some of them are slow and use a lot of memory (and still some people will use them). So knowing these properties will make it easier to find out which data structure you can use. In essence, there are a few questions you should ask when using a data structure:

- How fast is it to find elements sequentially?
- How fast is it to find elements randomly?

- How fast is it to add or remove elements?
- How much memory does the structure need?

But terms like "fast" or "much" are ambiguous terms. What do we mean by "fast"? Faster than a train or faster than a speeding bullet? Can we talk in terms of milliseconds? And if so, doesn't that differ per computer? So we must have an unambiguous way to define these terms.

Speed is Relative

Let's pretend for a second that PHP does not understand associative arrays and only uses numerical ones. This could be an example on how we could implement our own associate array class:

```php
class associateArray {
   protected $_elements;
   function set($key, $value) {
      $this->_elements[] = array($key, $value);
   }
   function del($key) {
      $index = $this->_findIndex($key);
      if ($index !== null) {
         unset ($this->_elements[$index]);
      }
   }
   function get($key) {
      $index = $this->_findIndex($key);
      if ($index !== null) {
         return $this->_elements[$index][1];
      }
      return null;
   }
   function _findIndex($key) {
      foreach ($this->_elements as $index => $value) {
         if ($this->_elements[$index][0] == $key)
               return $index;
      }
      return null;
   }
}
```

```php
$a = new associateArray();
$a->set("key1", "value1");
$a->set("key2", "value2");
print_r($a->get("key2")) . PHP_EOL;
print_r($a->get("not-existing-key")) . PHP_EOL;
```

In this example, we store our key and value together inside a numerical array. When we need to find a (alphanumeric) key, we iterate over the array, until we find a match. When found, we return the information on that specific index. But can we say that finding an element inside our class is "fast?"

We cannot define whether or not this method is fast by the number of milliseconds it takes. This would not be a very good way, since my laptop isn't running on exactly the same speed as yours, so when I say: "my findIndex() method of my associateArray class is 50ms fast," that doesn't say anything about how fast it will run on your system.

Also, its speed depends on how many elements there already are inside the array. It will run much faster with only 10 elements than with ten thousand elements since in the worst-case scenario the _findIndex() method would need to iterate over ten thousand items!

Just like Einstein did with his general relativity theory, we too will define speed as a relative term and we don't call it speed but "complexity." The complexity of a method (or algorithm, or data structure) measures how (and how much) it will be slower or faster when the number of elements used changes.

Let's take a close look at our _findIndex() method. What would happen when we already have 10 elements stored in our object? In the worst case scenario, where the element we need to find is the last element or the element does not exist inside the array, we need to loop over all the 10 elements. But when we have 100 elements, we need to loop over 100 elements. The more elements we have inside our object, the more time it takes for _fetchIndex() to complete. This time is proportional with the number of elements inside our object. Twice the amount of elements means

it will take twice the amount of time. We write this in shorthand as $O(n)$.
The "(n)"-part means a linear complexity: doubling the amount of elements
means doubling the time spent in this function.

Now let's take a look at the `set()` method. The only thing it does is add
an element at the end of the array. Let's assume for now, that adding an
element to the end of a numerical array takes just as much time when
we have 10 elements present in the array as when we have one million
elements. In that case, the `set()` function also doesn't take longer when
more elements are present inside the object. Since we don't need to loop
over already present elements, the time it takes always stays the same.
The time-complexity is in this case constant and we write this as $O(1)$.
This method doesn't get slower (or faster) when it needs to deal with more
elements. It is just as fast in adding an element when it already has stored
one or one million elements. Therefore: the complexity is constant.

The big-O notation only defines the complexity in the worst case scenario.
The best case scenario is a different situation. In our example, the best
case scenario when we are looking for the element is that that element is
the first element inside the array. In that case we always have to deal with
looking at only 1 element, the BEST case complexity is constant. We call
this the Big-Omega notation, as is denoted as $\Omega(1)$. When both the best case
complexity and the worst case complexity are equal, it can also be written
as Big-Theta: $\Theta(1)$.

A function that has a complexity of $\Theta(n)$, will in both the best case and the
worst case (or actually, in ANY case) run in linear time.

So in total we have defined three symbols defining complexity:

- O the worst case scenario for an algorithm
- Omega (Ω) the best case scenario for an algorithm
- Theta (Θ) the worst and best case are equal

But most of the time we will only talk about O, since it makes more sense to
talk about the worst case scenario instead of the best case to select our data
structures. The Ω and Θ aren't used that much in our cases.

Different Complexities

So now that we know about complexity, we can define different complexities. This actually is very difficult, but to make things easier for us programmers, we can place most of our functions into a small set of very common complexities. The complexities that I will describe next are sorted from the "best" to the "worst" kind of complexity.

Constant Time

Notation: `O(1)`

A constant time complexity means that no matter how many elements you have to deal with, the algorithm itself doesn't get slower (or faster). It is a constant algorithm.

Since complexities are generally a trade-off between time and space, a constant time function will almost always use more memory that other "more complex" functions. Many functions can be rewritten into `O(1)`, but the amount of code and memory usage will be too high for this to be considered practical.

Note that constant-time does not imply that it will be the fastest method (in milliseconds). Again, big-O notation does not specify absolute speeds, it specifies complexity. A `O(1)` function can be slower than a `O(n)` function with many elements. But because of the complexity, we know for a fact that given enough elements, the `O(1)` function will be faster after a certain amount of elements. It's up to you to decide whether or not your data structure or algorithm will ever reach that point.

Logarithmic Time

Notation: `O(log n)`

When adding elements to logarithmic algorithms, the first ones added result in a fairly high increase of time, but as even more elements are added, the additional increase in time is still there, but it is in increasingly smaller amounts, and therefore has a lesser impact as the quantity increases. This means that algorithms in `O(log n)` perform less efficient with only a few elements but they will perform better with many elements when compared to, for instance, linear complex algorithms.

In the graph below, you will see this line as a relatively vertical line that curves horizontal, indicating the less impact when dealing with many elements. This complexity is common when dealing with tree-like data structures as we will see later on.

Linear

Notation: `O(n)`

A linear complex algorithm has a constant increasing line. With 10 items, the algorithm will take twice as long as with five items. The same is true with 100 items, which will take twice as long as with 50 items. In a graph, you will see this line as a straight line sloping up. `O(n)` complex methods are easily spotted when you loop over elements with `foreach()` or other means.

Quadratic

Notation: `O(n^2)`

A quadratic function is easily identified by algorithms that need to loop over the same set of elements twice:

```
for ($i=0; $i!=$n; $i++) {
    for ($j=0; $j!=$n; $j++) {
        ...
    }
}
```

Some less optimized sorting algorithms use this complexity to sort items. As you can imagine, they are not really efficient when it comes to sorting a lot of elements. With 10 elements, we will loop the inner loop 100 times, with 100 elements; this already has grown to 10.000 times! As you can see, you have to be careful when doing this. It's very easy to create a simple algorithm that will check which elements are unique (for every element, we must iterate all other elements).

When developing software, always make sure that you test with a representative data-set. A $O(n^2)$ might not attract your attention when dealing with maybe 10 elements (for instance, blog posts that you need to sort), but as soon as you hit 1000 elements, those bottlenecks can grind your application to a halt.

Always make sure that you have at least a ballpark figure on your complexity, and if it's too high, decide whether or not that can become a problem. Then, and only then, you are in the business of writing scalable code.

Polynomial

Notation: $O(n^c)$

Most of the complexities above are already examples of polynomial complexities. The $O(1)$, which is mathematically the same as $O(n^0)$ $ (something to the power of 0 equals 1). $O(n)$ which is the same as $O(n^1)$ and quadratic, which is $O(n^2)$. A polynomial complexity can be seen as $O(n^c)$, where the 'c' is a constant. The higher this number, the steeper the line on and more expensive the algorithm will become when adding new elements.

Polynomial functions can be identified by a straight line on the graph below.

Exponential

Notation: $O(c^n)$

Exponentially complex algorithms can be seen as the opposite of logarithmic $O(\log n)$ functions. They start out quite efficient with only a few elements, but the more elements we add, the higher the cost will be per added element. This means that adding five elements to such an algorithm with already using 10 elements isn't as costly as adding five elements when it already contains 100 elements.

Think of it this way: Suppose we want to be able to store (large) numbers. We do this by actually storing the characters 0 to 9. If we use only one character, we can store the numbers 0 to 9. When we add another character, we can already store the characters 0 to 99. Adding a third will enable us to store the number 0 to 999. As you can see, the amount of numbers we can store by adding each character will grow exponentially.

This complexity can be very tricky for many developers. Since this complexity has no problem handling small data sets, developers who only test against small data (for instance, doing something with only 10 users) will never see any problems with the algorithm: it's very fast and doesn't look like a bottleneck. However, in production, where the amount of users reaches 1000 very quickly, the exponential algorithms become a bottleneck. And every user added to the system results in an even heavier load.

In the graph, you can see this complexity as a curved line that starts out horizontal and creeps toward vertical.

Factorial

Notation: $O(n!)$

The exclamation mark above serves two purposes. First, it's the mathematical notation for factorial, and the other purpose is to warn you that whenever you hit this complexity you should lookout for something else!

Having a function with a factorial complexity is usually a recipe for disaster. It's not something you like to have inside your application but on some occasions, you cannot avoid them.

You can calculate the factorial of a number by multiplying every number ranging from 1 to that number. This means that $4!$ equals

`1 * 2 * 3 * 4 = 24`. This doesn't look very high, but `10!` already is over 3.6 million, and `11!` is very close to 40 million.

Another one: `20!` would be around 2,430,000,000,000,000,000, which is, well, not a very small number to begin with. Thus the result: when your algorithm runs in 1 millisecond for 1 element, it will take the algorithm with 20 elements to run: 77 MILLION years (and will probably hit your `max_execution_time` before that).

But sometimes factorial algorithms cannot be avoided (yet). One of the most famous factorial examples is solving the traveling salesman problem through a brute force search. As you can image, even with 20 elements, solving this problem with brute force is nearly impossible.

Schema of All Big-O Complexities

This diagram shows you the different Big-O complexities. The higher the line, the longer the function will take. The bottom are the number of elements. As you can see, `O(2^n)` will rise up to the top immediately,

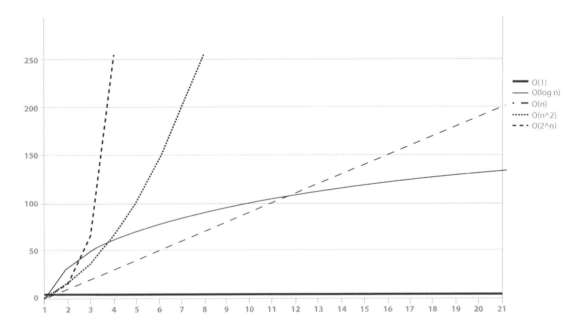

Figure 2.1

while the $O(1)$ never moves vertically (obviously, since the complexity is constant)

As you can see in Figure big-oh-complexity, a $O(2\char`^n)$ complex function doesn't necessarily have to be slower than a $O(\log\ n)$ function, but given enough elements, it will at some point. If you are sure you never reach that point, or you know that the time spent above this line is short enough, it's wiser to have a "slower" function than trying to reach for the less complex function all together.

What Does It All Mean

Code complexity, factorials, and polynomials; what does all this mathematical mumbo-jumbo have to do with me as a programmer?

Well, if you can identify the complexity of the algorithms used in your data structures, you can determine if the structure is actually useful for your purposes or not. If you know you a need a structure that needs to hold a lot of elements but in which you would never need to randomly seek, it might make more sense to use an SplDoublyLinkedList structure than a normal PHP array. It would save a lot of memory and still retain the speed for your need (adding elements to the back, and reading elements sequentially).

We're still not quite ready to talk about the SPL data structures yet. There is still another thing I'd like to discuss before moving to the SPL: the hash table.

> It's better to be safe and use PHP arrays, than to pick the wrong (SPL) data structure in your application.

This data structure is one that PHP uses internally for their arrays and lots of other things. This data structure is a very good compromise between memory usage and time and it works quite well in almost all cases. Both sequential and random reads are very fast which; is not something every data structure is able to do.

On the whole, the standard data structure internally used by PHP's array is quite all right for most purposes. This also makes it true that when you are in doubt about which data structure to use, the PHP array is always a good choice.

PHP Internal Hash table

So PHP arrays are internally stored as a data structure called a hash table. It is called a hash table because internally, all elements are located through "hashes". The key of an element is converted to a hash so the structure knows where to find the element.

To actually store these elements, the hash table uses "buckets", which are just storage containers that can store one (or more) elements. A bucket-list is a block of memory that stores the pointers to those buckets. This way we can quickly find the correct bucket in memory if we know the bucket-number (this is important to keep the data structure fast).

Before we can add our data into the buckets, we must know which data goes into which bucket. To do this, the hash table uses the key of the data, and creates a hash value of that key. The algorithm used is called DJBX33A which returns a bucket number (a number between 0 and the number of buckets that are currently available in this hash table).

Now that we have found the bucket inside the bucket-list, we can look up or store the element inside that bucket.

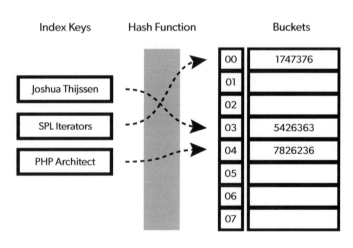

Figure 2.2

In essence, what happens when fetching an element is this:

- hash the key to a bucket index
- find the bucket inside the bucketlist by jumping directly to the bucket index
- fetch and return the element from that bucket

As you see we do not need to iterate over any element and everything works with constant time complexity ($O(1)$). It does not matter how many elements or buckets there are inside the hash table: the time to fetch ANY item will remain constant.

Hash Collisions

Sometimes it will happen that two keys will result in the same bucket-number. This is known as a hash-collision. What happens when something is already present inside the bucket is that it will add the new element after that element. So in effect, there will be two elements residing in the same bucket which are linked together (through a doubly linked list, which we will talk about later on).

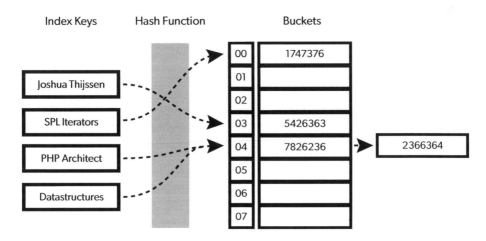

Figure 2.3

When fetching one of these elements, the algorithm detects that there are more elements inside the same bucket, and will look at the first element to see if that element is the one we need. If not, it will look at the second one etc., until the correct element has been found. This means that the complexity has changed from $O(1)$ into $O(n)$, where "n" stands for the number of elements inside that bucket (which is not the same as the number of elements inside the complete hash table!).

Obviously, this takes time so we like to avoid hash-collisions as much as possible since it will slow down operations, but we can never avoid them. The DJBX33A algorithm used for hashing the indexes to bucket numbers is chosen because it generates very few collisions.

Memory Usage

When a hash table is initialized, a bit of memory will be allocated for internal usage and for some variables you probably will be adding. But since arrays in PHP are dynamic, it might be possible that we want to add more elements than it initially has allocated. In that case, it will allocate more memory for the hash table by doubling the number of elements that it can store (it will double the amount of buckets). Initially it provides room for 8 elements and when that number is reached, it will double it to 16. Once we hit 16 elements, it will double to 32, 64, 128 etc. until we reach the maximum of 2147483648 elements (this is even true for 64 bit environments) which is the theoretical maximum number of elements you can store inside an array in PHP.

But this limit is really a theoretical limit because for every element you want to store, you also need some memory that holds the value of that element; and storing this number of elements will make you run out of memory. In fact, to store only a half percent of elements (around 10 million elements), you would need around 2GB of memory.

But changing the number of buckets of a hash table comes with an expensive price: since the hash function returns a number between 0 and the number of buckets, it might be possible that a key will end up in another bucket. For instance, the key "foo" might end up in bucket 6 when the hash table has 10 buckets, but when it uses 20 buckets, it might end up in bucket 15. Therefore, ALL the elements inside the current hash table must be "rehashed" to the correct buckets. And as you can imagine, it means iterating over all the elements, which is an $O(n)$ operation: the more elements inside the array, the longer it will take for the rehashing to complete.

Performance

As said earlier, this hash table data structure is a pretty good compromise between speed and size. The complexity of the functions to update this data structure is good enough for most purposes. At the end of this chapter, I've included a table with all the data structures, operations and their complexities. This also includes the PHP array (or actually the underlying hash table data structure).

Because it is such an efficient structure, it's not strange that PHP uses this hash table data structure internally to store all kinds of data, like the properties and methods of classes, your globals variables, your include files, etc.

Introduction to SPL Data Structures

Chapter 3

Available SPL Data Structures

In this chapter, we will discuss all the SPL data structures that are currently available in PHP v5.4. Some of them are based on other data structures, for instance, the `SplMinHeap` and `SplMaxHeap` are extended classes from the `SplHeap` while `SplStack` and `SplQueue` are extended from `SplDoublyLinkedList`.

All these data structures implement the `Iterator` and `Countable` interface, which means all data structures are countable (`count()` will return the number of elements inside the structure) and they are traversable with `foreach()`, but not every structure is really fitting for iteration as I will show you later on.

Most of them also implement the `ArrayAccess` interface so they can also be used as an array by accessing elements through `[]`. For more information about these interfaces, take a look at the chapter about the SPL interfaces where they are discussed in detail.

SplDoublyLinkedList

Before we can talk about what doubly linked lists are, we first have to know what "normal" linked lists are. As the name implies, it's a data structure where elements are linked together. Every element in the list has at least two properties: a pointer to the actual data that is stored and a pointer to the next element in the linked list.

The only thing we need to remember is the first element (usually called the "head"). When we need to find an element, we start by looking at the head. If that element isn't the one we need, we use the pointer to go to the next element. We continue this process until the pointer of an element doesn't points to null. In that case, we have found the "tail" element, or the last element of the linked list. When creating a linked list, usually both the head and tail elements are stored as meta-data for quicker access.

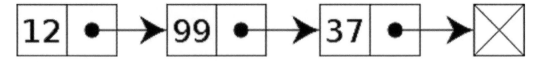

Figure 3.2

Adding and Deleting Nodes

Inserting a new element is nothing more than changing the pointer of the previous element to let it point to the new element, and have the new element point to the next element.

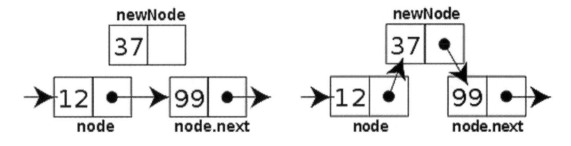

Figure 3.3

Available SPL Data Structures

Deleting is more or less the same but has a drawback when it comes to single linked lists: if we want to delete element N, we need to have access to element N−1. This is because we need to point element N−1 to element N+1, which in effect, skips the element N. Therefore the delete method must look up the N−1 element by searching this element from the "head" element. To overcome this problem, a lot of single `LinkedList` structures have a `deleteAfter`, where you do not point to the element you need to delete, but to the element before that.

Sequential reads are very fast with linked lists. Since we can just read the "head" element, and move up until we have reached the "tail" element, we don't need special methods like we needed to read hash tables sequentially. However, random reads on linked lists are usually slower: if we need to read the 6th element, we need to fetch the "head" element and move up 5 elements before we have found the 6th element. This implies that random reads have a $O(n)$ complexity, while sequential reads have a $O(1)$ complexity.

Double-Linked Lists

A double-linked list is nothing more than adding an additional pointer to each element. This pointer points to the PREVIOUS element. This means that from every element we can either move forwards or backwards which speeds up a lot of things.

Deletions are much easier. Since we know we want to delete element N, we can move one element backwards to find the previous element, and one element forward to find the next. The delete operation has become a $O(1)$ complex operation which, written in PHP code looks like:

```
protected function delete(dllElement $element) {
    dllElement $previous = $element->prev;
    dllElement $next = $element->next;
    $previous->next = $next;
    $next->previous = $previous;
    $element = null;
}
```

Random reads would still not be possible, but sequential reads from back to front are made easy.

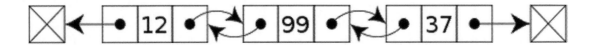

Figure 3.4

Advantages of Using Linked Lists

One of the properties of linked lists is that they don't need to have a fixed size. A linked list can be empty, or can hold thousands of elements. We do not need to allocate any memory in advance, which is something that we need to do with hash tables (otherwise they would be too slow). This makes linked lists very memory efficient data structures with very fast insert/delete capabilities. Merging lists is easy as well: just connect the tail of linked list 1 to the head of linked list 2, and you're done.

Counting Elements

Even though a lot of operations can be done in $O(1)$, not all of them are. Random reads aren't $O(1)$, but also counting elements is not easy. It implies that we have to count all elements by iterating from the head to the tail, which again is a $O(n)$ ($o(n)$). Because counting is such a common thing to do, PHP has added additional meta-information such as the number of elements, which is stored inside the linked-list. This means that counting the elements inside a linked list (SplDoublyLinkedList::count()) is $O(1)$ as well, but merely by cheating.

Usage

SplDoublyLinkedLists is a perfect way to save memory while still being able to use (most) array functionality. Its main purpose is to iterate over elements in a sequential way, either forwards or backwards. Do not

Available SPL Data Structures

use this data structure when you are planning to do mostly random reads.

Notable Methods

void setIteratorMode (int $mode)

The `setIteratorMode` defines how they behave during iteration of the list. The following constants can be set:

- IT_MODE_LIFO - The elements are read last in-first out. In other words: read backwards.

- IT_MODE_FIFO - The elements are read first in-first out. In other words: read forwards like a normal iterator. This is the default mode.

Additionally, you can OR the above values with either one of these:

- IT_MODE_KEEP - Elements are kept when iterating (default behavior).

- IT_MODE_DELETE - When iterating, the elements are automatically deleted.

If you need to have a last-in first-out list where items are deleted, you should use the `IT_MODE_LIFO|IT_MODE_DELETE`. The default mode is `IT_MODE_FIFO|IT_MODE_KEEP`.

mixed bottom (void)

This will return the "head" or the first element that has been added to the list.

mixed top (void)

This will return the "tail" or the last element that has been added to the list.

void unshift (mixed $value)

Unshifting a value means it will be added to the "head" of the list. This is different from the normal insert method `push()`, where it will be added to the "tail" of the list.

mixed shift (void)

`shift()` does the opposite of `unshift()`: it will remove an element from the head of the list.

SplStack

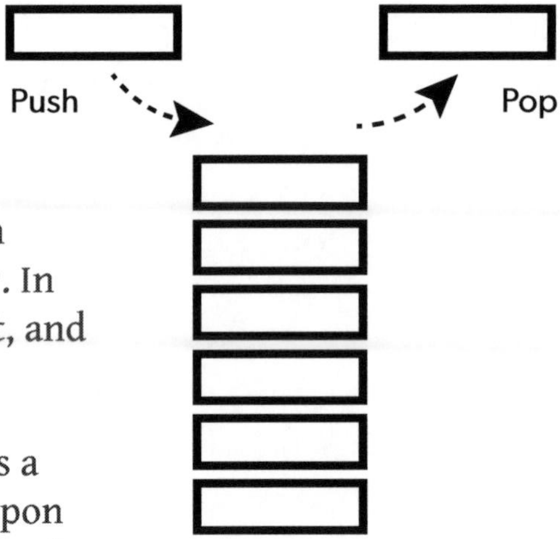

As you will see with other SPL data structures, most of them are not really different from each other. An `SplStack` is not much more than an `SplDoublyLinkedList` with an iteration mode of `IT_MODE_LIFO|IT_MODE_KEEP`. In other words: we can traverse last in-first out, and elements are NOT removed when iterating.

A stack is just a linked list, but can be seen as a vertical list, where elements are "stacked" upon each other. The usage of a stack is that you work with the last element that has been `push()`'ed

Push

Pop

Figure 3.5

onto the stack before you move to underlying elements (you can iterate through the stack though, but it wouldn't really be a stack anymore).

It is possible for you to change the mode to `IT_MODE_DELETE`, but you cannot set the mode to `IT_MODE_FIFO`. It will throw a `RuntimeException` if you do. That makes sense because otherwise it wouldn't be a stack, but a queue.

For all purposes, this structure is completely the same as an `SplDoublyLinkedList`, it even shares the same internal codebase inside the PHP core.

Usage

Use an `SplStack` when you need to store data, but you only need to deal with the last element stored. This is mostly useful for recursive functionality where you store elements onto the stack and deal with them, until the stack is empty again. Since this class extends the `SplDoublyLinkedList`, it inherits all the drawbacks and benefits of that class.

Notable Methods

void setIteratorMode (int $mode)

You can only set the mode to either `IT_MODE_LIFO|IT_MODE_DELETE` or `IT_MODE_LIFO|IT_MODE_KEEP`. It's not possible to set to `IT_MODE_FIFO` since that would turn the `SplStack` into an SplQueue and therefore will result in a `RuntimeException`.

void SplDoublyLinkedList::push (mixed $value)

`push()` 'ing a new element means a new element is appended to the "tail" of the stack.

mixed SplDoublyLinkedList::pop (void)

`pop()` 'ing is the opposite of pushing an element. It will remove the last element from the stack and return it to the user. If there are no more elements to pop, it will throw a `RuntimeException` (even though an `UnderFlowException` would have made more sense).

Usage Example

This example creates a calculator that uses stack-based operations. It creates an SplStack where we push an operation and 2 operators onto the stack. The operators by themselves can also consist of an operation and 2 operators. This way, we can create a nested "formula" that a very easy recursive function can calculate. It only takes two operators and the operation from the stack, does the calculation and pushes the result back onto the stack. It will continue this process until only one item (the actual result of the formula) is present.

```
$stack = new SplStack();

// This will calculate: (((3 * 4) + 4) - 2) / 2) = 7
$stack->push("divide");
$stack->push(2);
$stack->push("subtract");
$stack->push(2);
$stack->push("add");
$stack->push(4);
$stack->push("multiply");
$stack->push(3);
$stack->push(4);
calculate($stack);

print "The result: ".$stack->pop() . PHP_EOL;
exit;

function calculate(SplStack $stack)
{
    $value1 = $stack->pop();
    $value2 = $stack->pop();
    $cmd = $stack->pop();

    // Execute command and push the result back onto the stack
    switch ($cmd) {
        case "add" :
            $stack->push($value1 + $value2);
            break;
        case "subtract" :
            $stack->push($value1 - $value2);
            break;
        case "multiply" :
            $stack->push($value1 * $value2);
            break;
        case "divide" :
            $stack->push($value1 / $value2);
            break;
    }

    // If we still have multiple entries on the stack,
    // so calculate again
    if ($stack->count() > 1) {
        calculate($stack);
    }
}
```

Available SPL Data Structures

splQueue

The `SplQueue` also shares much of the codebase from `SplDoublyLinkedList`. A queue however, can be seen as a standard `doublyLinkedList`. Queues are mostly used for adding data at the back, and reading data from the front (or the other way around, if you prefer that). Just like a queue in your local supermarket, the first one in the queue will be the first one out of the queue.

So in order to mimic queues, this class has two additional methods: `enqueue()` and `dequeue()`. These methods are nothing more than aliases for respectively `SplDoublyLinkedList::push()` and `SplDoublyLinkedList::shift()` but they provide more sensible names when it comes to dealing with queues.

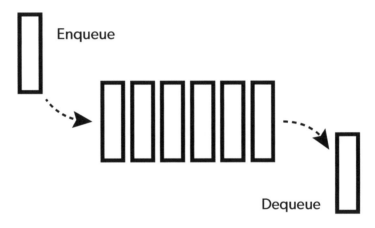

Figure 3.6

Because it's a queue, it comes with a default iterator mode of `IT_MODE_FIFO|IT_MODE_KEEP`. We cannot change the iterator-direction through the `setIteratorMode()` method call. The mode is always `SplDoublyLinkedList::IT_MODE_FIFO` (as opposed to `SplStack`, where it's `SplDoublyLinkedList::IT_MODE_LIFO`). Only the `IT_MODE_KEEP` can be changed to `IT_MODE_DELETE`.

Usage

Use `SplQueue` when you need to deal with data that you need to store, but want to fetch in the same order. Because it is implemented as an `SplDoublyLinkedList`, it inherits all the drawbacks and benefits of that class as well.

Notable Methods

mixed dequeue (void)

A simple alias to the `shift()` method. They are interoperable, but it makes more sense to use `dequeue()` when dealing with queues.

void enqueue (mixed $value)

A simple alias to the `push()` method. Again, it makes more sense to use this method.

Usage Example

This example creates an "eventhandler" where you can hook your own functions into. Note that we are using `isEmpty()` and the `dequeue()` methods instead of a `foreach()` loop, otherwise it wouldn't be a real queue. Another problem that would occur is that when another method adds a new function to our queue, the `foreach()` can get corrupted. If you deal with stacks and queues, always use them in the way they are intended.

```
/**
 * Using a queue to add events to an event handler
 */

$eventHandler = new SplQueue();
$eventHandler->enqueue("function1");
$eventHandler->enqueue("function2");

while (! $eventHandler->isEmpty()) {
    $event = (string)$eventHandler->dequeue();
    if (function_exists($event)) {
        $event($eventHandler);
    }
}
```

Available SPL Data Structures

```
function function1(SplQueue $eventHandler) {
    print "Function 1 called. " .
          "Adding function3() to the event handler\n";
    $eventHandler->enqueue("function3");
    $eventHandler->enqueue("a message for function 3");
}

function function2(SplQueue $eventHandler) {
    print "Function 2 called.\n";
}

function function3(SplQueue $eventHandler) {
    $msg = $eventHandler->dequeue();
    print "Function 3 called. Message: $msg\n";
}
```

SplHeap

The `SplHeap` is a data structure where an element is inserted directly into a sorted position within certain conditions. For instance, when we have the elements 10 and 20 inside a heap, the element 15 would be inserted in between those two elements. This could be done through a simple (double) linked list, but we run into problems: every time you insert a new element, it has to scan all the elements until it finds the correct position. Worst case scenario (when it has to add the element to the back of the list), it would mean it's a `O(n)` complex algorithm.

However, the `SplHeap` uses a binary tree with a heap property which means that most operations have a complexity of `O(log n)` instead of `O(n)`. At the end of the chapter, I'll explain in depth how this binary heap works internally.

The `SplHeap` is the first data structure we encounter that isn't based on `SplDoublyLinkedList`. This structure however cannot be used directly since it's an abstract class. The class has one abstract method you need to define: `compare()`. This function will compare two elements, and should return a positive number (normally, 1) if `value1` is greater than `value2`, a 0 when both values are equal, and -1 or any other negative number when `value2` is greater than `value1`. What defines "greater" is up to your own heap class. You could be comparing numbers, strings, the Greek alphabet where "omega" > "alpha", or anything else you want. My friend Michelangelo van Dam has posted an example of a `SplHeap` class that automatically adds Belgium soccer clubs and their rankings to the heap, which are automatically inserted at the correct location of their rank. It basically sorts while you insert the elements, which can be much quicker than inserting all the elements, and then performing a sort. You can find this example in the PHP documentation at: http://php.net/class.splheap. php.

Dealing with SplHeap Corruptions

When the compare method is called while inserting or deleting elements, and something happens during the compare method and an exception is thrown, the `SplHeap` can end up in an unknown state. All heap read/write methods from that point on will throw a `RuntimeException` saying the heap is corrupted.

Since something happened during the `compare()` method, SplHeap cannot guarantee that the heap is sorted in the way you have intended, but sometimes it is possible to recover. For instance, by regenerating the heap or re-adding the elements (in the hope that `compare()` doesn't throw an exception this time).

Before you can do this, you must "unblock" the `SplHeap` in order for you to add elements. This is done by the `recoverFromCorruption()` method. It's a bit of a misnomer really, since it doesn't do anything to recover from the corruption, but merely releases the flag that tells the SplHeap that it's corrupted (internally represented by the `SPL_HEAP_CORRUPTED` flag).

But in all fairness: when something has happened, your best choice is to deal with the `RuntimeException` thrown by the `SplHeap` and don't recover from the heap at all. Instead, re-throw the exception or don't catch the exception at all.

Available SPL Data Structures

Dealing with Same Value Elements

It's possible to add elements with the same value multiple times inside the `SplHeap` but this is not recommended. There is no reason to assume that the order is the same as the order in which they are added to the heap so if you need specific ordering of the elements with that same value, you must use another way to deal with this problem.

Iterating the SplHeap

One very important aspect when dealing with an `SplHeap` is that whenever you `extract()` or iterate the `SplHeap` with `foreach()`, you are in essence destroying the `SplHeap`. This makes the data structure less useful for multiple iterations like you can do with the `SplDoublyLinkedList`.

Notable Methods

abstract int compare (mixed $value1 , mixed $value2)

This method must be overridden when extending the `SplHeap` class. It will be called by the `insert()` method when a new item is entered into the tree. Depending on the output of this method, it will decide where to store this item.

As a result, it must return a positive number when `$value2` is larger than `$value1`, a negative number when `$value1` is larger than `$value2` and a zero when `$value1` equals `$value2`. Best practice is to return either a +1, -1 or 0. This is the most common way of returning values in many comparison functions in both PHP and other languages, but returning other values might be easier on occasion.

Usage Example

This example orders an array of names and ages according to age. The person who is the oldest will be on top. In order to make this work, we have created a new class that extends `SplHeap` and implemented a `compare()` method that compares ages against each other. This allows the heap to decide where in the tree the element will be stored.

The compare method subtracts the 2 ages from each other. This results in a positive, negative or 0 value. So in our example, we ignore the best practice advice I stated above.

```php
class AgeHeap extends SplHeap {
    protected function compare($value1, $value2)
    {
        return $value1['age'] - $value2['age'];
    }
}

$ageHeap = new AgeHeap();
$ageHeap->insert(array('name' => 'joshua', 'age' => 33));
$ageHeap->insert(array('name' => 'esther', 'age' => 30));
$ageHeap->insert(array('name' => 'lisanne', 'age' => 5));
$ageHeap->insert(array('name' => 'marij', 'age' => 53));
$ageHeap->insert(array('name' => 'skoop', 'age' => 30));

// Print result
foreach ($ageHeap as $item) {
    print $item['name']." is ".$item['age']." year old"
        . PHP_EOL;
}
```

How SplHeaps Works Internally

The `SplHeap` is implemented as a binary heap. This can be visualized as a tree structure where every element (called the node) has a maximum of two child nodes. Also, it's not possible for one leaf to have two or more extra leaves than others. Its shape is balanced, also known as a complete binary tree. Depending on the comparison method you implement, either

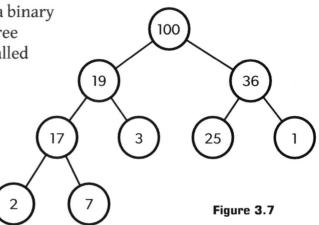

Figure 3.7

every child node is greater than or equal to, or lesser than or equal to its parent node. This is an example of a binary tree representation where every child node is greater than or equal to its parent
(See figure 3.7).

This representation of a tree must be implemented in code. This is done through a standard block of continuous memory which can be seen as an array. (Note that this is not the same as a PHP array, which is implemented as a hash table).

Index 0 of our array always returns the top item of the heap. In this case it holds the value 1. Because we are using a balanced binary tree, the following conditions are always met:

- Children of index N are located at: `a[2n+1]` and `a[2n+2]`.

- Parent of index N is located at `a[floor(n-1)/2]`.

So for example, the parent of node 7 (index 3) is located at $3-1/2 = 1$. The value of index 1 is 5, which is its parent. The children of index 1 (value 5) are $2*1+1 = 3$ and $2*1+2 = 4$ thus, value 7 and 9. This is how internally a binary tree structure is stored inside a continuous block of data.

Inserting an Element

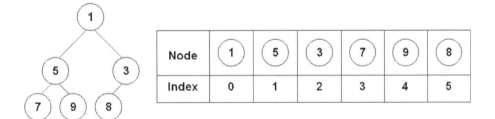

Figure 3.8

Inserting an element is not hard, but requires a bit of work. What we do is add the element to the end of the array, in a sense adding it to the last leaf of the tree. If there isn't enough room, the `SplHeap` will allocate more memory by doubling the memory block. After we have added the item, it might not be at the correct position. We could very well have added the value "2" to our heap, so in the tree shown above, node 3 would have "8" and "2" as its children. This is not correct, since parents should always be less than the children in our case.

In order to fix this, we do a so-called "bubble-up" process. We compare the node with its parent. If it's less, we swap the elements. We continue this process for every node we swap, until the parent is less.

In our case, it would look something like this:

Index	0	1	2	3	4	5	6
Node	1	5	3	7	9	8	2

The parent of index 6 is index 2 (`floor(6-1)/2`). The value of index 2 is a "3".

Value "3" is greater than our value "2". We swap these values.

Index	0	1	2	3	4	5	6
Node	1	5	2	7	9	8	3

Parent of index 2 is index 0 (`floor(2-1)/2`). The value of index 0 is a "1".

Value "1" is less than our value "2". We can stop.

At this point, we have successfully bubbled up and the tree is balanced again. One of the major benefits of this is that we only need to deal with one path inside the tree. The more items stored inside the tree, the deeper the path will become. But every time we need to add more items to the tree in order to get to the next deeper level. This results in the effect that inserting an element has the complexity of `O(log n)`.

Deleting the Top Item

Deleting an item is only possible for the top item, or the root-node. Deleting this item is not really difficult, but when we delete the root node, we end up with 2 separate trees. So instead we do the following:

We fetch the last item in the array (the last inserted node) and move that to the root node. If that node is larger than one of the child-nodes, it has to "bubble-down". This is done by swapping the element with one of the children. This is done until both children are smaller than the parent, in which case the tree is balanced again.

The Downside of Heaps

So heaps are very efficient in adding data that will be automatically be sorted. However, there are some drawbacks when using heaps. For one: it's not really possible to iterate over the elements. You CAN do this, but you can never assume an order. Another issue, it's not possible to do random reads: fetching the 5th element is not possible since we don't know where to look. The only thing we know for sure is that the top (first) element is the highest element.

SplMaxHeap

An `SplMaxHeap` is nothing more than an `SplHeap` class in which the `compare()` method has been implemented. Its main purpose is to provide a heap where the highest element is always on top. Comparing is done internally through the `compare()` function, but you can override this function if needed.

There are some things to consider when comparing elements:

- Comparing null against null results in an equal comparison.
- Comparing null against a Boolean (`true`) will result in Boolean(`true`) being larger, otherwise, they are equal.
- Comparing a Boolean(`true`) against null will result in

Boolean(true) being larger, otherwise, they are equal.

- Boolean(true) is larger than Boolean(false)

- When comparing a string with null, it will internally compare the string against an empty string (string(0) "").

- An object is always larger than null.

- When comparing arrays, the array with the least amount of elements is the smallest. On the same amount of values, the elements are checked in order.

Usage Example

This example generates a series of strings and adds them to the maxHeap. It will print out the strings ordered from highest to the lowest by comparing characters.

```php
$maxHeap = new SplMaxHeap();
for ($i=0; $i!=10; $i++) {
    // Generate a string between 5 and 10 characters long
    $str = randomString(rand(5,10));
    $maxHeap->insert($str);
}
foreach ($maxHeap as $str) {
    print $str . PHP_EOL;
}
exit;
// Generates a random string from the letters 'A' to 'Z'
function randomString($len = 10) {
    $str = "";
    while ($len > 0) {
        $str .= chr(rand(ord('A'), ord('Z')));
        $len--;
    }
    return $str;
}
```

SplMinHeap

An `SplMinHeap` is the opposite of `SplMaxHeap`. Its main purpose is to provide a heap where the lowest element is always on top. As with the `splMaxHeap`, the class extends from the `SplHeap` where only the `compare()` method has been changed.

Usage

Use this class when you need a heap that automatically orders elements in an ascending order. Since this class extends from `SplHeap`, all operations have the same complexity as `SplHeap`.

Usage Example

This example is a somewhat "strange" way of dealing with `minHeaps`. This is a simple way of distributing elements evenly over a series of arrays. At first, we insert 10 empty arrays into the `minHeap`. Then, we retrieve the lowest value (the array with the least amount of values), and insert an element to that array. Because that array is now "larger" than others, when we retrieve again the lowest value from the heap, it will be another array, so we add another element to that one. This in effect will distribute the elements evenly over all the arrays inside the heap without strange ways like looping or counting.

```php
$minHeap = new SplMinHeap();

// Fill the heap with empty arrays that are going
// to be filled
for ($i=0; $i!=10; $i++) {
    $minHeap->insert(array());
}

// Continuously add items to the top entry
for ($i=0; $i!=100; $i++) {
    // Extract top item from the heap
    $item = $minHeap->extract();
    $item[] = rand(1,99);
    // Insert back into the heap
```

```
    $minHeap->insert($item);
}

// Print result
foreach ($minHeap as $item) {
    foreach ($item as $k) printf ("%2d ", $k);
    print PHP_EOL;
}
```

SplPriorityQueue

The `SplPriorityQueue` is a nice way of dealing with elements that have an "external" priority. It is not based on the `SplHeap` class, but internally it does share most of its functionality. It has the same problems like corruptions happening when exceptions are thrown during `compare()` methods, and thus it has the same `recoverFromCorruption()` method as well.

But the `SplPriorityQueue` is different in a way that is useful when you need to deal with external values. Suppose you have elements, but those elements by themselves cannot be compared, but they are compared through external information. For instance, when you have a logging system, you want to place all your log messages inside a queue so other systems can read the messages first in-first out. However, some messages are more important: a message indicating that your disk space is about to run out should have a higher priority than a message that indicates that somebody has successfully logged into your application.

With the help of the `SplPriorityQueue`, you can add these messages to a queue, but it will move elements that have a higher priority up to the front of the queue, and elements with a lower priority to the back.

When you are handling the queue, elements that have a high priority will come first, all the way down to the lowest priority elements. When you add elements to the queue through the `insert()` method, you add an additional $priority. This value will be used for comparison to find out where in the list the element needs to be inserted.

Usage

The `SplPriorityQueue` is useful when dealing with data which uses an external method of prioritizing. If the data itself contains the priority (for instance, a "Person" class can be prioritized by its property `$age`), you should use either `SplMinHeap`, `splMaxHeap` or create your own class by extending `SplHeap`. Internally it uses the same structure as `SplHeap` so all element operation complexities are similar to that of the `SplHeap`.

Notable Methods

int compare (mixed $priority1 , mixed $priority2)

This method will be called when inserting a new element. It will compare two priorities to find out where the new element will be placed. There is no reference to the actual element, just the priority. It should return either a negative or positive value (-1 and +1 are the most common values), or 0 when both priorities are equal.

void insert (mixed $value , mixed $priority)

This will insert a value inside the heap based on the priority. If there are items of the same priority already present inside the heap, the order in which the element is placed is undefined: if you have 5 elements with a priority 1, there is no guarantee that the first element from that priority will be the first element added. If there is a new element added, it might also change the order again. In order words: if ordering matters, make sure you use a different priority, or a different data structure.

void setExtractFlags (int $flags)

Because the `SplPriorityQueue` needs to remember the priorities in order to add new elements, it's also possible to extract those priorities again. The `setExtractFlags()` method defines what gets returned by the `top()`, `extract()` and `current()` methods:

- EXTR_DATA - Returns the data. This is the default behavior.

- EXTR_PRIORITY - Returns the priority instead of the data.

- EXTR_BOTH - Returns an array with the data and priority. The array is an associative array with the keys 'data' and 'priority'.

Usage Example

This example creates a simple logging system that prioritizes log messages. These priorities are defined as ERROR, WARNING and NOTICE for the sake of clarity.

When we handle our queue, we don't use a standard foreach() loop, but we use a `while()` loop and isEmpty() to check for pending messages. We use the extract() to fetch the first message waiting (the one with the highest priority). During the loop if we add other messages to the queue, we are still able to parse them correctly. When using a foreach() loop, things would get messy when adding new elements during the loop.

```php
// Define priorities for logging
define('ERROR',   9);
define('WARNING', 5);
define('NOTICE',  1);

$logQueue = new SplPriorityQueue();
$logQueue->insert(
    "Somebody has logged into the system", NOTICE);
$logQueue->insert(
    "Disk space is almost empty", ERROR);
$logQueue->insert(
    "Somebody tried to log in 3 times with the wrong password"
    , WARNING);

while (! $logQueue->isEmpty()) {
    $message = $logQueue->extract();
    print $message . PHP_EOL;
}
```

SplFixedArray

The fact that PHP stores arrays inside a hash table has both advantages and disadvantages. The advantage is efficiency: to read and write to the array is pretty quick but this comes with the price of a bit higher memory usage.

Another benefit is that PHP arrays are associative arrays. You can use strings as keys without any additional penalties.

However, sometimes you need to push the limits of PHP arrays to the max when it comes to both performance and memory usage. For instance, when dealing with a large list of elements and doing operations on those elements. In that case, SplFixedArray might be of interest to you.

SplFixedArrays will speed up operations on the array, and decreases memory usage at the same time. In other words: you can do more or faster, while using less memory. As a penalty though, you will not be able to use it as an associative array: you can only use numeric values for indexing.

Another drawback: you have to decide upfront how many elements will be stored inside your array. This value has to be set during the construction of SplFixedArray objects. If you know you will store a maximum of 10 elements, you just create an SplFixedArray of 10 elements.

Note that you have to be careful when using count() functions. It will not return the number of elements that are filled, but the actual size of the array (which makes sense, in a way).

```php
$phpArray = array();
$phpArray[5] = "foo";
$fixedArray = new SplFixedArray(10);
$fixedArray[5] = "foo";
print "phpArray size: " . count($phpArray) . PHP_EOL;
print "fixedArray size: " . count($fixedArray) . PHP_EOL;
```

This will output:

```
phpArray size: 1
fixedArray size: 10
```

Even though the array size is fixed, there is still a way to increase or decrease the size if needed. For instance, when you have a fixed array of 10 elements, increasing it to 20 elements is just a matter of calling the setSize() method:

```
$fixedArray = new SplFixedArray(10);
print "fixedArray size: " .
count($fixedArray) . PHP_EOL;
$fixedArray->setSize(20);
print "fixedArray size: " .
count($fixedArray) . PHP_EOL;
```

> **Note that resizing can be quite a performance bottleneck when dealing with large amounts of elements.**

will result in a size of "10" and "20". Decreasing is also possible, but values that will fall outside the range will be removed (and might get destructed as well):

```
class testClass {
    function __destruct() {
        print "Destructor called!" .
            PHP_EOL;
    }
}
$obj = new testClass();
$fixedArray = new SplFixedArray(10);
$fixedArray[8] = new testClass();
$fixedArray->setSize(5);
print "Done with resizing the array" . PHP_EOL;
```

When you run the code, you will see that after scaling down the array from 10 to 5, it will automatically remove (and destruct) our object, since it is on index 8.

Notable Methods

SplFixedArray::fromArray()

This static method makes it easy to convert a PHP array to an SplFixedArray. Note that the PHP array must not contain alphanumeric keys, only numeric keys are allowed otherwise SplFixedArray::fromArray() will throw an InvalidArgumentException.

This method takes into account the actual indexes. For instance, the following code will produce a fixed array with a size of 6:

```
$a = array("foo", "bar", 5 => "baz");

$fixedArr = SplFixedArray::fromArray($a);

print "The size of the array is : "
    . $fixedArr->getSize() . PHP_EOL;
print_r ($fixedArr->toArray());
```

If you don't want this to happen, you can set the second argument of `fromArray()` method to `false`. In that case, it will ignore the keys from the PHP array and uses its own numbering when creating the fixed array.

SplObjectStorage

The `SplObjectStorage` data structure is a two-for-the-price-of-one structure. It's a very simple structure - internally represented by a "normal" hash table, just like the PHP array, but it's a very useful structure to be used as a set or as a map.

A map, sometimes called a dictionary, is similar to the PHP's associative array: you can use alphanumerical keys to store information. If you want to store the objects as keys, you must "hash" them to a unique value. This can be done by the `spl_object_hash()` function. But this would mean the object would get hashed twice: once by `spl_object_hash()` and once when adding to the hash table.

The `SplObjectStorage` allows you to directly add an object as a key without hashing it manually. In effect hashing only occurs once (internally when storing). This can lead to performance improvements, especially when dealing with a large amount of objects.

But the `SplObjectStorage` also can be used for "sets". A set is a simple storage container where you can store elements without any order. One of the main advantages is that you can quickly and easily test if elements are present inside a set, but it isn't really used for retrieval of that data.

This structure uses more memory than a standard array, but the main advantage for using this structure is for the additional methods on maintaining the contained objects. It has optimized methods for adding, removing and seeking objects inside the container, as well as all kinds of "set" functionality like removeAll(), addAll() and removeExcept().

Another benefit is that objects are stored only once inside the container. When you want to add an object that is already stored inside the container, it will not store it again.

```
$obj1 = new StdClass();
$obj2 = new StdClass();
$obj3 = $obj1;  // Reference to the same object

$container = new SplObjectStorage();
$container->attach($obj1);  // Gets stored
$container->attach($obj2);  // Gets stored
// Does not get stored, since it's the same as $obj1
$container->attach($obj3);

print "There are ".count($container) . " objects stored." .
    PHP_EOL;
```

This will output "There are 2 objects stored" since both obj1 and obj2 are different instances of the object, but obj3 is a reference to obj1. Since this object is already present, it will not be added again.

However, through the help of the getHash() method (available since PHP version 5.4), you can control on what and how to add containers. For more information, see the getHash() explanation in the "Notable methods" section below.

Usage

Use this class when you need to maintain a (large) set of objects. Since this class is internally represented by a hash table, there are no immediate benefits of using this class versus the standard PHP array. However, this class has some optimized and specific functionality when it comes to dealing with maintaining objects.

Notable Methods

public void attach(object $object [, mixed $data = NULL])

This method will attach an object to the storage, accompanied with some additional data. When the exact same object already is present in the storage, it will not insert the object, but overwrite the old object. This has no effect on the object itself (since they are the same physical object), but when you have additional data, the old data will be overwritten by this new data.

public void addAll (SplObjectStorage $storage)

Adds all objects from the `$storage` object storage into this one. It basically acts as a merge between the two storages. Note that objects that are already present inside the destination storage will have their additional data overwritten just like the `attach()` method.

public void removeAll (SplObjectStorage $storage)

This method will remove all objects that are attached to the `$storage` object storage. It can be seen as `array_diff()` functionality.

public void removeAllExcept (SplObjectStorage $storage)

This method will remove all objects inside the storage that are NOT present inside the `$storage` object storage.

public mixed getInfo (void)

This will return the data that accompanies the object and which can be set by either `setInfo()` or as the `$data` parameter in the `attach()` method. Note that this method will fetch the data from the object that the `current()` is pointing to. As with the `current()` and `key()` methods, this method only works AFTER you have called `rewind()`, otherwise the internal pointers are set incorrectly.

public void setInfo (mixed $data)

The `setInfo()` method allows you to modify the data of the object that the storage currently points to. It works the same way as the `getInfo()` method, so these methods only make sense inside loops where you iterate over the objects inside the storage.

public string getHash (object $object)

This method returns the hash of the given object. This internally calls the `spl_object_hash()` function so the result of both functions is the same. However, you can override this method to use your own "hashing" functionality.

This allows you to decide, based on your own logic, whether or not the object must be added to the storage.

The next example will only allow you to store objects that are from different types. Even though the objects by themselves are different, the types are not, so they don't get added:

```php
class MyStorage extends SplObjectStorage {
    function getHash($object) {
        return $object->type;
    }
}

$obj1 = new StdClass();    $obj1->type = "foo";
$obj2 = new StdClass();    $obj2->type = "bar";
$obj3 = new StdClass();    $obj3->type = "foo";

$tmp = new MyStorage();
// Type is "foo"
$tmp->attach($obj1);
// Type is "bar"
$tmp->attach($obj2);
// Not added: other object but same "type" as obj1
$tmp->attach($obj3);
```

Usage Example

This example is a very basic way of dealing with objects. It implements the Observer design pattern which allows you to add listening objects, so-called observers, to an object that is called the "subject". We achieve this by creating a `$_listeners` object storage that holds all our listeners. Because we can only add every object once, it will automatically deal with trying to add the same observer multiple times.

```php
class MySubject implements SplSubject {
    protected $_listeners;
    public function __construct() {
        $this->_listeners = new SplObjectStorage();
    }
    public function attach(SplObserver $observer) {
        $this->_listeners->attach($observer);
    }
    public function detach(SplObserver $observer) {
        $this->_listeners->detach($observer);
    }
    public function notify() {
        foreach ($this->_listeners as $observer) {
            $observer->update($this);
        }
    }
    public function getObserverCount() {
        return count($this->_listeners);
    }
}
class MyObserver implements SplObserver {
    public function update(SplSubject $subject) {
    }
}
$obs1 = new MyObserver();
$obs2 = new MyObserver();
$obs3 = new MyObserver();
$subject = new MySubject();
$subject->attach($obs1);
$subject->attach($obs2);
$subject->attach($obs2);
$subject->attach($obs3);
$subject->attach($obs1);
print "There are " . $subject->getObserverCount()
    . " observers attached." . PHP_EOL;
```

Available SPL Data Structures

Code Complexity of the SPL Data Structures

This table gives you an overview of the complexities for the most common operations on the data structures found in the SPL. I've included the PHP array as well as a reference. As I've said before: the downside of faster, less complex algorithms is that the memory usage will be higher. That's why you shouldn't judge the data structure merely on its complexity.

Structure	Insert Element at the Beginning	Insert Element at the End	Insert Element in the Middle	Delete Element from the Beginning
SplDoublyLinkedList	O(1)	O(1)	O(n)	O(1)
SplStack	O(1)	O(1)	O(n)	O(1)
SplHeap[1]	O(log n)	O(log n)	O(log n)	O(log n)
SplPriorityQueue[1]	O(log n)	O(log n)	O(log n)	O(log n)
SplFixedArray	O(1)	O(1)	O(1)	O(1)
SplObjectStorage	O(1)	O(1)	O(1)	O(1)
PHP Array[2]	O(1)	O(1)	O(1)	O(1)

[1] It's not possible to random read a heap structure, but they are automatically sorted.

[2] When a hash collision occurs, it will need to traverse a double linked list. Also, they need to be resized every time new memory has to be allocated out.

Available SPL Data Structures

Structure	Delete element from the end	Delete element from the middle	Sequential read	Random reads
SplDoubly-LinkedList	O(1)	O(n)	O(1)	O(n)
SplStack	O(1)	O(n)	O(1)	O(n)
SplHeap	O(log n)	O(log n)	O(log n)	-[1]
SplPriorityQueue	O(log n)	O(log n)	O(log n)	-[2]
SplFixedArray	O(1)	O(1)	O(1)	O(1)
SplObjectStorage	O(1)	O(1)	O(1)	O(1)
PHP Array	O(1)	O(1)	O(1)	O(1)

[1] It's not possible to random read a heap structure.

[2] When a hash collision occurs, it will need to traverse a double linked list. Also, they need to be resized every time new memory has to be allocated out.

Available SPL Data Structures

Available SPL Data Structures

Chapter 4

Iterators

Even though technically the "iterator" itself isn't part of the SPL, iterators in the PHP world probably have become famous thanks to the SPL. This is because the SPL is mainly known for its large set of iterators. And even though they have strange names like IteratorIterator, or even RecursiveIteratorIterator, they all do serve a purpose. This chapter introduces you to all the SPL iterators, what their functions are and how to use them with the help of some examples.

In order to understand how the iterator interface works, please take a look at the interface inside the "SPL Interfaces" chapter. To reflect the layout of the PHP.net manual, this chapter comes after this iterator chapter, and also discusses some other non-SPL interfaces like the "IteratorAggregate" and "Traversable".

What Are Iterators?

What exactly is an iterator? In a sense, it's an object that allows you to traverse elements inside that object. Something like this is already possible with any object: if you do a `foreach()` loop over an object, it will return its public properties. But true iterators are much more powerful. They can be used to return ANY kind of values, not only the

> Iterators are PHP's way of dealing with abstracting away the traversal logic from the business logic. This, in one sentence, sums up what an iterator is.

properties. So they provide a much better way of controlling what (and how) to return values and it makes it easier for programmers to deal with business logic without worrying too much with the traversal logic.

Creating your own iterator in PHP is easy. You only have to implement the "Iterator" or the "IteratorAggregate" interface. Technically, you need to implement the "Traversable" interface, but this is a sort of internal interface that cannot be extended by your own PHP code. This "Traversable" interface is implemented by the "Iterator" and "IteratorAggregate". Your code will throw an error when you implement the "Traversable", but I'd reckon it's something you should have done at least once your life.

Why Use Iterators?

"Why use iterators when you can also use arrays?" It's a simple question but with a not-so-simple answer.

To answer your question, let's take a look at a code snippet that will print all the files from the current directory:

```
$dir = opendir(".");
while (($file = readdir($dir)) !== false) {
    print "file: $file\n";
}
```

Many programmers will use something very similar to this snippet. It will open the directory, and for as long as `readdir()` will return a filename, it will print that filename: Very simple.

Now let's assume that you need to add another feature: you need to display files in the directory, but only when they end with the ".mp3" extension.

Again, we could modify our code a bit:

```
$dir = opendir(".");
while (($file = readdir($dir)) !== false) {
    if (! preg_match('|\.mp3$|i', $file)) {
        continue;
    }
    print "file: $file\n";
}
```

The `preg_match()` checks if the filename ends in .mp3 (case-insensitive) and if not, it will continue with the loop. If it matches, the file will print.

But extending this loop comes with a price. What would the code look like if you need to search for all image files (which end in .GIF, .JPG and .PNG for instance), or for .MP3 files that are larger than 4MB in size?

What would happen if we sometimes want to change what we want to filter, depending on some configuration settings or wishes from the end-user?

In the end, this code will have three main disadvantages:

- The code isn't maintainable.
- The code isn't reusable.
- The code isn't testable.

Maintainable software is important. It allows you to easily add updates or check for bugs without having to spend too long figuring out how and what the code is doing in the first place. Reusability allows you to use the same piece of code on multiple occasions. If you hardcoded a match for MP3 files, you cannot use the code for finding JPG or GIF images. You must either copy/paste most of the code and change the extensions to look for; or create a function that will allow an argument to be passed with an array of extensions to look for. But it would not matter if you also need to look for files larger than a certain size, or older than a certain age. In the end, you cannot really reuse this method; otherwise it would become unmaintainable with all the if-statements and special cases you would need to build. And last, but not least, you cannot really test this code. You could test input against output, but you cannot really test specifically each component or know what is wrong when the test fails.

Solving the Problem with Iterators

Let's solve the same problem with iterators. First, the easy task of finding all files in the directory:

```
$it = new DirectoryIterator(".");
foreach ($it as $file) {
    print "File: ".$file->getPathname()."\n";
}
```

This code looks cleaner. There are no strange loops, just a simple `foreach()`. Next up: filtering on filenames.

```
$it = new DirectoryIterator(".");
$it = new RegexIterator($it, "/.mp3$/i");
foreach ($it as $file) {
    print "File: ".$file->getPathname()."\n";
}
```

Do you see how we haven't change anything in our previous code, we just added a new iterator (a `FilterIterator` to be exact) OUTSIDE the `foreach()` loop? This iterator will only return values that match the regular expression (since this is a `RegexIterator`).

Let's go crazy and only return at most the first three MP3 files in our directory:

```
$it = new DirectoryIterator(".");
$it = new RegexIterator($it, "/.mp3$/i");
```

```
$it = new LimitIterator($it, 0, 3);
foreach ($it as $file) {
   print "File: ".$file->getPathname()."\n";
}
```

Again, there is no change, just an extra iterator in the chain. From this point, we can add every type of functionality by chaining more iterators. You can either use the standard SPL iterators, or create your own by extending some of the base iterators like the `FilterIterator`.

So what have we achieved?

- The code is maintainable. We don't have to change our main loop. That always stays the same. The filtering of elements is done outside this loop. It's easy to see what is happening without any conditional statements.

- The code is reusable. We could put our main loop in a function that would accept any iterator as a parameter. In that case, we can use this main loop for filtering out files any way we want.

- The code is testable. We can isolate the DirectoryIterator to check it's resulting values, we can isolate the RegexIterator to check if it returns items according to the regular expression. This isolation makes unit testing of the code possible.

Another great advantage is that we have separated our business logic (doing something with the filtered files) and our filter logic. It results in less bugs, easier to read code and thus makes your life as a programmer (and more importantly, the guy that needs to maintain your code) much better.

Since iterators are just plain objects over which you have full control, you can let that object decide how data is stored. It could either store all data directly into the iterator (like the ArrayIterator), you can fetch the data when it's needed (like a SQL-cursor) or a hybrid, that caches the result inside the iterator for faster retrieval when the data is needed again (more or less, what a CachingIterator can do). On occasion, this makes it easier and quicker to work with iterators instead of arrays, while it is still possible to maintain most of the array functionalities, including the adding and indexing through the `[]` operators.

I hope at least you find that using iterators can be very helpful in many ways. In fact, there aren't that many reasons left for you to use standard arrays for iteration-purposes!

Creating Your Own Iterators

Creating your own iterator is very easy. The only thing you need to do is implement the five methods from the Iterator interface: `key()`, `current()`, `rewind()`, `next()` and `valid()`. More "complex" iterators can also implement other interfaces like `SeekableIterator`, `Countable`, `Serializable` and `ArrayAccess` for instance.

Depending on your needs, you can decide if your iterator has all its data in memory (like an array), or if the data will be fetched or calculated when needed in the `current()` method. Both have their pros and cons. For instance, "cursors" (like SQL record iterators) normally have only one record in memory, and when iterating, it will fetch a new record every time. This way we don't have to keep all data records.

To see the difference, let's take a look at an "AlphabetIterator", which lets us iterate over the characters 'a' to 'z'.

```
class AlphabetIterator implements Iterator {
   protected $_current;
   protected $_key;
   public function rewind() {
      $this->_current = 'a';
      $this->_key = 1;
   }
   public function current() {
      return $this->_current;
   }
   public function key() {
      return $this->_key;
   }
```

```
    public function next() {
        $this->_current++;
        $this->_key++;
        return $this->_current;
    }
    public function valid() {
        return ($this->key() <= 26);
    }
}
$alphabet = new AlphabetIterator();
foreach ($alphabet as $position => $letter) {
    echo $position . ' => ' . $letter . PHP_EOL;
}
```

We have never defined a full set of the characters 'a' to 'z'. The current returns the correct character by "calculating" this on the fly.

First of all, you will see that we start with a key index of 1 instead of 0. This is because I'd like to think that the first letter in the alphabet is 'a'. From a programmer's point of view, the alphabet would probably range from 0 to 25 instead of 1 to 26.

The next() method does nothing more than increasing the $_current property, which returns the current letter. Our valid() method will check to see if our key() value is less than or equal to 26. If so, it means we are still in our alphabet. Once we hit index 27, we know we have finished and it will return false which in turn stops the foreach() loop.

Chaining Iterators

To show you how easy it is to use filtering through iterators, we add a simple iterator that will filter out the vowels from our alphabet:

```
class VowelFilterIterator extends FilterIterator {
    public function accept() {
        return in_array($this->current(),
            array('a', 'e', 'i', 'o', 'u'));
    }
}

$alphabet = new AlphabetIterator();
$vowels = new VowelFilterIterator($alphabet);
foreach ($vowels as $position => $letter) {
    echo $position . ' => ' . $letter . PHP_EOL;
}
```

We didn't have to change anything in our `foreach()` loop (I've modified the iterator name from `$alphabet` to `$vowels` for clarity though), and we didn't have to modify anything in our `AlphabetIterator`. It still returns the complete alphabet but it's the decorating `VowelFilterIterator` that decides if the current value is accepted or not. Our filter accepts only the values that are actual vowels, and those values are actually used in our foreach. By "chaining" iterators you have a very flexible and efficient way of managing your data.

The FibonacciIterator

The next iterator is the `FibonacciIterator` which iterates over the Fibonacci sequence. A Fibonacci sequence is the sequence of numbers where every number is the sum of the 2 previous ones. This sequence starts like this: 0, 1, 1, 2, 3, 5, 8, 13, 21, 34, 55.

```
class FibonacciIterator implements Iterator {
    protected $_previous;
    protected $_current;
    protected $_key;
    public function rewind() {
```

```php
        $this->_previous = 1;
        $this->_current = 0;
        $this->_key = 0;
    }
    public function current() {
        return $this->_current;
    }
    public function key () {
        return $this->_key;
    }
    public function next() {
        $old_current = $this->_current;
        $this->_current += $this->_previous;
        $this->_previous = $old_current;
        $this->_key++;
        return $this->_current;
    }
    public function valid() {
        return true;
    }
}
$fibonacci = new FibonacciIterator();
foreach ($fibonacci as $number) {
    echo $number . ', ';
}
```

The Fibonacci sequence iterator does not use a predefined sequence.
It's just an ongoing stream of Fibonacci numbers and you see again, this
iterator "generates" its element, rather than traversing an internal list of
elements.

The next() method calculates the next Fibonacci number (by adding
the previous number to the current number). The valid() method
always returns true, which means there is no stopping this sequence.
However, PHP cannot handle very large numbers (numbers higher than
the PHP_INT_MAX constant), so after a while it will return "inf" instead of
actual numbers.

If you want to limit the sequence you can filter it as well. For instance, you want to return the first 50 Fibonacci numbers. In that case you can use the `LimitIterator` to limit your actual dataset:

```php
$fibonacci = new FibonacciIterator();
$fibonacci = new LimitIterator($fibonacci, 0, 50);
foreach ($fibonacci as $key => $number) {
    echo $number . ', ';
}
```

Again, the only difference is that we add another iterator. There are no changes needed in the Fibonacci iterator itself, or in the `foreach()` loop.

The SPL Iterators

We've already covered a few SPL iterators: the `LimitIterator`, the `FilterIterator` and the `DirectoryIterator`, but there are many more. The SPL defines many iterators that can be used directly or can be used as a base which can be extended to do almost everything you want to.

It's quite interesting to see that internally, the SPL iterators are all pretty similar. Most of the SPL iterator codebase is shared among all iterators, with only a few exceptions. Most of the functionality is based on extending only one or two methods, which hints to a good and robust object-oriented foundation on which the SPL is built.

> Most of the iterators are in fact modeled from iterator classes written in PHP, which can still be found inside the PHP source code: https://github.com/php/php-src/tree/master/ext/spl/internal

AppendIterator

The `AppendIterator` is an iterator that "combines" multiple iterators together. This can be very useful if you have multiple iterators that you cannot connect easily in another way; for instance, `DirectoryIterators` from two different directories, or result sets taken from multiple databases or multiple queries. By appending those iterators with the `AppendIterator`, you can still use those different results as if they came from one iterator.

public void append (Iterator $iterator)

This method appends a new iterator. Note that it is possible to append the same iterator multiple times. This is different from - for instance - the `MultipleIterator`, where you can attach every iterator only once. This is because the `AppendIterator` internally uses the `ArrayIterator` for storage, while `MultipleIterator` uses `SplObjectStorage`, which doesn't allow multiple references to the same object.

public void getArrayIterator (void)

Returns the internal `ArrayIterator` that the `AppendIterator` keeps with all the appended iterators.

public void getInnerIterator (void)

Returns the iterator that the `AppendIterator` currently is iterating.

public void getIteratorIndex (void)

Returns the current iterator index. If you have appended multiple iterators, this method will return which iterator index (starting from 0) we currently are iterating.

Note that the `AppendIterator` works by "switching" iterators that are internally stored. This means that the `key()` returns the key value of the iterator that is internally used for iterating. This means that you must be careful when expecting a sequential key numbering. I've written a possible solution by creating a "merge"-iterator that returns a sequential key index (and thus ignoring the original keys). You can find this blogpost at http://www.enrise.com/2010/12/appending-the-appenditerator/.

Example

This example "concats" two separate directories into one single iterator that can be used for traversing.

```
$it = new AppendIterator();
$it->append(new DirectoryIterator("/dir"));
$it->append(new DirectoryIterator("/other/dir"));
foreach ($it as $item) {
   print $item . PHP_EOL;
}
```

ArrayIterator

This iterator is probably the most known iterator. It's a common way to convert an array into an iterator (so actually the opposite of the `iterator_to_array()` function). The biggest disadvantage of this iterator is that the actual data is always stored inside the iterator rather than fetched whenever needed.

Note that this iterator does not iterate recursively. For that you need the `RecursiveArrayIterator()`.

All standard array functionality, like `count()` and using `[]` is implemented as well so this iterator mimics pretty much "normal" arrays.

> There is not much to gain when it comes to either memory or speed if you convert arrays to iterators. If you need the speed and/or memory, take a look at the SPL data structures.

The `ArrayIterator` supports a series of sorting methods that allows you to sort the outcome of the iterator. These methods (`uasort()`, `natcasesort()`, `asort()` etc.) are the equivalent of the same standard array functions.

public array getArrayCopy (void)

This method returns a copy of the iterator as an array. So in a sense, it's the same as performing an `iterator_to_array()` call. Since PHP arrays and the internal storage of the data inside the ArrayIterator are both using a hash table data structure, creating the actual array is not very time consuming.

public void setFlags (void)

There are two flags that you as a user can set to control the way properties are handled inside an ArrayIterator.

- STD_PROP_LIST - Properties set to the iterator are not added to the iterator-array.

- ARRAY_AS_PROPS - Properties set to the iterator are set to the iterator-array.

They sound like they are mutually exclusive, but setting only the STD_PROP_LIST does not have any effect. To understand the difference, check out the following example:

```
$it = new ArrayIterator();
$it['foo'] = "bar";
```

This would set the "foo" index to "bar" just like you would set an index inside an array (or anything that implements ArrayAccess). Let's see what we can do when the ARRAY_AS_PROPS is set:

```
$it = new ArrayIterator();
$it->setFlags(ArrayIterator::ARRAY_AS_PROPS);
$it->foo = "bar";
```

This would also set (or overwrite) the "foo" index but we are referring it as a property. If you are going to do this, the flag ARRAY_AS_PROPS MUST be set. If you forget this, PHP will not add the property to the actual internal storage.

```
$it = new ArrayIterator();
$it->setFlags(ArrayIterator::ARRAY_AS_PROPS);
$it->foo = "bar";
print_r($it);
$it = new ArrayIterator();
$it->foo = "bar";  // This is incorrect now
```

```
print_r($it);
$it->baz = "qux";
```

Which will return:

```
ArrayIterator Object
(
    [storage:ArrayIterator:private] => Array
        (
            [foo] => bar
        )
)
ArrayIterator Object
(
    [foo] => bar
    [storage:ArrayIterator:private] => Array
        (
        )
)
```

You see how the "foo" property is inside the storage on the first iterator, and outside on the second. A subtle difference, but an important one nevertheless.

Example

This small example creates an iterator that iterates over all letters of the alphabet.

```
$alphabetIterator = new ArrayIterator(range("A", "Z"));
foreach ($alphabetIterator as $v) {
    print "V: $v" . PHP_EOL;
}
```

CachingIterator

The CachingIterator is a strange iterator. It combines three different kinds of functionality into one iterator.

The first feature is that the iterator will read the next value into memory before it is needed. In effect it would mean that the current() is always "one" behind the actual iterator. This is very useful in order to find out if the iterator has more items available. This is not always possible since not every iterator has `count()` functionality, like iterators that read from streams.

But the `CachingIterator` is much more than a simple lookahead iterator. Its second feature is that it is possible to let the iterator "cache" all the values it returns. This is extremely useful when you are dealing with iterators that take a long time to fetch or calculate elements. Every time an item gets fetched, it will be stored inside an internal cache. When you need to fetch older elements, you can fetch them from `getCache()` or through the standard `[]` functionality provided by the `ArrayAccess` interface. Note that you can only fetch items that are already seen by the iterator. If you have iterated over 5 elements, it's not possible to fetch the eighth, for instance.

The third feature of the `CachingIterator` is the most complex one and deals with how it can be cast to a string. Normally this would be done through the magic `__toString()` method. But you can control what the `CachingIterator` actually casts to a string. The flags `CALL_TOSTRING`, and the `TOSTRING_USE_*` flags control how this is used. They are described below.

public void hasNext (void)

This will return true when there is another element inside the iterator. It will return false when no more items are available. Useful to use in functions when you want to know if we are reaching the end of the iterator, without leaving the `foreach()` loop.

Flags

The `CachingIterator` has multiple flags which can be set through the constructor, or by the `setFlags()` method.

- `CALL_TOSTRING` - Will call the standard `__toString()` method when the `CachingIterator` is cast to a string. It works just like a regular cast would work.

- CATCH_GET_CHILD - This flag is not used inside the CachingIterator.

- TOSTRING_USE_KEY - Returns the current key when casting the CacheIterator to a string.

- TOSTRING_USE_CURRENT - Calls the inner iterator's __toString() when casting the CacheIterator to a string.

- FULL_CACHE - This will enable the getCache() method and stores all values inside an internal array.

  Bitmasked flags should only be set through the | (OR) operator. If you set multiple flags with +, you might get unexpected results (that is to say, unexpected for you).

Note that the CachingIterator might be confusing when it comes to its flags. There are many things you have to look out for:

- You can only use getCache() and array functionality though [] when you have set the FULL_CACHE flag.

- You cannot set TOSTRING_* functions together with CALL_TOSTRING.

- Once you have set the CALL_TOSTRING or TOSTRING_USE_INNER flags, you cannot unset them. This would result in an exception.

- When you unset the FULL_CACHE flag, it will clear the currently set cache.

- When TOSTRING_USE_INNER flag is set, you must make sure that the inner iterator also provides a __toString() method.

- The iterator does not automatically use its internal cache when iterating multiple times.

Example

This example will show you how the iterator can be used as a "lookahead" iterator.

```
$alphabetIterator = new ArrayIterator(range("A", "Z"));
$it = new CachingIterator($alphabetIterator);
foreach ($it as $v) {
    if (! $it->hasNext()) {
        print "And this is the last letter of the alphabet: ";
    }

    print "$v" . PHP_EOL;
}
```

This example shows how the caching works. After the initial iteration, the cache will be filled with an array of letters. We use the array access method through [] to fetch the item from the cache. It will not have called the internal ArrayIterator to find the index.

```
$alphabetIterator = new ArrayIterator(range("A", "Z"));
$it = new CachingIterator($alphabetIterator,
                          CachingIterator::FULL_CACHE);
foreach ($it as $v) {
    // Do something with the iterator
}

// Fetched from the cache, not from the internal
    ArrayIterator
print "The fourth letter of the alphabet is: ". $it[3] .
    PHP_EOL;
```

CallbackFilterIterator

The callbackIterator is a FilterIterator that allows you to provide a callback mechanism for every item that needs to be filtered. You can provide a callback function (or closure) through the constructor which gets called during accept(). This function is useful when you need a filtering method that doesn't deserve its own filterClass. Most of the time, you would provide a

Be careful with the parameters in your callback function: the first parameter is $current, the second one $key, which is the reverse of what one might expect. The third parameter is the actual iterator if you need to use it.

closure to the `CallbackFilterIterator`.

Example

This example uses a closure to select only files whose size is below 1024 bytes.

```
$it = new DirectoryIterator(".");
$it = new CallbackFilterIterator($it,
    function($current, $key, $iterator) {
        return ($current->getSize() < 1024);
    }
);

foreach ($it as $item) {
    print $item->getSize() . " "
        . $item->getFileName() . PHP_EOL;
}
```

DirectoryIterator

The `DirectoryIterator` is a `SplFileInfo` iterator. It will accept a directory which in return iterates it and returns `SplFileInfo` objects for each file found in the directory. Note that if you need to recursively iterate over a directory, you must use the `RecursiveDirectoryIterator` instead.

For more information about the items returned, take a look at the `SplFileInfo` chapter in this book.

SeekableIterator

This iterator implements the `SeekableIterator`. This means that we can use `seek()` to directly jump to a file inside our directory. Note that when jumping outside the range of the directory, it does not throw an exception, but merely returns an empty object.

```
$it = new DirectoryIterator("/my/dir");
// Assuming you have over 5 files in this directory.
$it->seek(5);
$item = $it->current();
```

Iterators

```
print $it->current()->getFilename() . PHP_EOL;
// Assuming you have less than 100 files in this directory.
$it->seek(100);
print $it->current()->getFilename() . PHP_EOL;
```

Dealing with Current()

There is a bit of a "problem" with the `DirectoryIterator`, which is something that has been pointed out on occasion, but can trick you into debugging code for a long time if not careful. Suppose you have the following code:

```
// Read directory and store SplFileInfo Objects
// for later use.
$it = new DirectoryIterator("/my/path");
foreach ($it as $f) {
    $files[] = $f;
}
// Now iterate over all the file objects
foreach ($files as $fi) {
    print $fi->getFileName() . PHP_EOL;
}
```

This might seem to work, but it doesn't do what you expect. Every file you see will be the last file in the directory! The problem lies in the fact that `DirectoryIterator::current()` returns itself (`$this`) as the current value. So when dealing with this in the first `foreach()` loop, this is not a problem. But remember how PHP 5 deals with copying objects: it really doesn't. What PHP does, is store the object identifier in our `$files` array, which is the same object identifier that is stored in `$f`. This also means that whenever you make a change to `$f` in our loop, it also changes the object you just stored in `$files`, since they are in fact both the same object in memory. But this is also true for `$f` as well: `$f` contains the current `SplFileObject` that gets returned by the iterator, but in fact it's just an object identifier to one single `SplFileObject` that is stored inside the iterator. In the `foreach()` loop, this `SplFileObject` gets reused (thus saving memory and gaining a speed performance), meaning that `$f` always points to the same object, and thus every `$files[]` element point to the same object!

You can easily test this for yourself by checking the object ID's:

```
// Read directory and store SplFileInfo Objects
// for later use.
$it = new DirectoryIterator("/my/path");
foreach ($it as $f) {
    print "Object id: " . spl_object_hash($f) . PHP_EOL;
    $files[] = $f;
}
```

Luckily, the answer to this problem is actually very simple: you need to clone() the objects if you are going to reuse them outside your iterator foreach() loop:

```
// Read directory and store SplFileInfo Objects
// for later use.
$it = new DirectoryIterator("/my/path");
foreach ($it as $f) {
    // Store a CLONE of $f, not actual $f itself.
    $files[] = clone $f;
}
// Now iterate over all the file objects, correctly:
foreach ($files as $fi) {
    print $fi->getFileName() . PHP_EOL;
}
```

Example

This example iterates a directory and returns information about the files.

```
$it = new DirectoryIterator("/my/dir");
foreach ($it as $item) {
    // Returns the name of the file
    print $item->getFilename() . PHP_EOL;
    // Returns the size of the directory which the
    // files contains
    print $item->getPathInfo()->getSize() . PHP_EOL;
    // Returns the size of the file
    print $item->getSize() . PHP_EOL;
}
```

EmptyIterator

An `EmptyIterator` is basically a dummy iterator. You can use it inside a `foreach()`, but never returns any values. The `valid()` method will always return false.

Calling the `current()` and `key()` methods directly will result in PHP throwing a `BadMethodCallException`, so don't call them.

This iterator can be used as a placeholder where you need to use an iterator, but don't have any data associated with it.

```php
$it = new EmptyIterator();
foreach ($it as $element) {
    // We never reach this, since the EmptyIterator
    // does not contain any elements
}
```

FilesystemIterator

The `FileSystemIterator` is an extension of the `DirectoryIterator`. This iterator is identical to the `DirectoryIterator`, but you can easily control the way keys and values are returned by this iterator. This is done by controlling the flags through either the constructor or through `setFlags()` method.

Flags

There are multiple groups of flags that can be set by either the constructor or by the `setFlags()` method. Note that all flags are bit-wise flags. The first group decides how the `key()` and `current()` methods act:

- `KEY_AS_PATHNAME` - Returns the path of the file as the key. Note that this can be a relative path if you have specified a relative path in the constructor.

- `KEY_AS_FILENAME` - Returns only the filename as the key.

- `CURRENT_AS_FILEINFO` - Returns the `current()` as an `SplFileInfo` object.

- `CURRENT_AS_PATHNAME` - Returns the `current()` as a pathname of the file. This can be a relative path if you have specified a relative path in the constructor.

- `CURRENT_AS_SELF` - **Returns the iterator (`$this`).**

- `NEW_CURRENT_AND_KEY` - Is an alias of

> Working with bitwise masks can be difficult when you are not used to it. I've written a blogpost about bit manipulation in PHP which you can find at http://www.adayinthelifeof.nl/2010/06/02/bit-manipulation-in-php/

```
KEY_AS_FILENAME | CURRENT_AS_FILEINFO
```

The second group decides how and which elements are returned:

- `SKIP_DOTS` - **Does not return the dot-files (. and ..) entries. Hidden Unix files (files starting with a .) will be returned normally.**

- `UNIX_PATHS` - **Will convert path separators to forward slashes (the Unix path separator). Useful when your code is running on a non-Unix system like Microsoft Windows.**

The last group is about masking the current and key flags:

- `CURRENT_MODE_MASK` - **When masked, it will only return the bits used for changing the** `current()` **behavior.**

- `KEY_MODE_MASK` - **When masked, it will only return the bits used for changing the** `key()` **behavior.**

* OTHER_MODE_MASK When masked, it will return all the bits that are not used for masking the current() and key().

Example

This example will return an array of the whole directory (except the dot-files) with the filename as the key and the `SplFileObject` as the value.

```
$it = new FilesystemIterator(".",
    FilesystemIterator::KEY_AS_FILENAME |
    FilesystemIterator::CURRENT_AS_FILEINFO |
    FilesystemIterator::SKIP_DOTS);
print_r (iterator_to_array($it));
```

FilterIterator

The `FilterIterator` is an abstract class that can filter out unwanted elements from any kind of iterator. This filtering is very powerful and allows you to "chain" multiple iterators together easily with each of them filtering out unwanted values. There is one abstract method you need to implement: `accept()`. This method will return a Boolean `true` when the item is allowed, or Boolean `false` when the item should not be returned by the iterator (and thus: filtered).

Because the FilterIterator needs the know the current() value before filtering, it doesn't help you in speeding up iterators that spend a lot of time generating or fetching the current() data. For instance, when your current() returns a record from the database, it must be fetched PRIOR to the filtering. Thus filtering would not help you to speed up this process.

The SPL does supply a few `FilterIterators` by itself but it's quite easy to create your own by either extending this class or creating simple closure-type filters with the `CallbackFilterIterator`.

Example

```
class SizeFilterIterator extends FilterIterator {
    protected $_size = 0;
    public function __construct(Iterator $iterator, $size) {
        parent::__construct($iterator);
        $this->_size = ($size < 0) ? 0 : $size;
    }
    public function accept() {
        $item = $this->current();
```

```
        if ($item instanceof DirectoryIterator) {
            return ($item->getSize() < $this->_size);
        }
        return strlen($item) < $this->_size;
    }
}
$it = new DirectoryIterator(".");
$it = new SizeFilterIterator($it, 1024);
foreach ($it as $item) {
    print $item->getFileName() . PHP_EOL;
}
```

This is a simple example that will filter "sizes". In our `accept()` function, we check if the given item is an instance of the `DirectoryIterator`. If so, it will check its file size. When it isn't a `DirectoryIterator`, it will simply check the length of the item (compatible with most iterators, since they provide a `__tostring()` method to convert the object to the string).

This means our iterator works just as easily with a non-`DirectoryIterator`:

```
$it = new ArrayIterator(
    array("Foo", "bar", "baz", "foobar", "barfoo"));
$it = new SizeFilterIterator($it, 4);

foreach ($it as $item) {
    print $item . PHP_EOL;
}
```

It's very easy to extend the iterator itself: we could supply a flag to see if the size needs to be checked with a "greater-than", or "less-than" option.

But adding if-statements to detect on what kind of iterator we are filtering can become unmaintainable very quickly. In those cases I would suggest looking at the `CallbackFilterIterator`, or maybe even use the following example:

```
class SizeFilterIterator extends FilterIterator {
    protected $_size = 0;
```

```
    protected $_cb = null;

    public function __construct(Iterator $iterator,
                                $size, Closure $cb = null) {
        parent::__construct($iterator);

        $this->_size = ($size < 0) ? 0 : $size;
        $this->_cb = $cb;
    }

    public function accept() {
        $item = $this->current();

        if ($this->_cb) {
            $cb = Closure::bind($this->_cb, $this,
                                'SizeFilterIterator');
            return $cb($item);
        }
        return strlen($item) < $this->_size;
    }
}
```

There is a bit of "magic" going on with the closure binding. This is available from PHP 5.4 only, and allows you to bind a closure to a specified object: In our case, the SizeFilterIterator. This way, when calling the closure, it acts like a method inside our object so we have access to our "_size" property, which otherwise wasn't available. It would also allow you to use other properties and methods that might be available inside the iterator if needed.

Now we could very easily provide a closure to the SizeFilterIterator so it knows how to check for size:

```
$it = new DirectoryIterator(".");
$it = new SizeFilterIterator($it, 1024, function($item) {
    return ($item->getSize() < $this->_size);
});
```

This would check against the file size. Since we know it will be a DirectoryIterator element, we don't have to perform this check like we had to do in our previous examples.

```
$it = new DirectoryIterator(".");
$it = new SizeFilterIterator($it, 15, function($item) {
    return (strlen($item->getFileName()) < $this->_size);
});
```

This example shows how you could easily switch from checking the file size to checking the file name size. In this example, we check if the filename is less than 15 characters. If so, it will pass; otherwise it will be filtered out.

FilterIterators are one of the most powerful iterator types around. They provide an easy way to filter out unwanted values, but with the help of closures and new PHP 5.4 functionality, they become even more powerful.

GlobIterator

The GlobIterator extends from FileSystemIterator so all functionality inside FileSystemIterator will also be available with the GlobIterator. Internally, it will use PHP's glob:_ stream-functionality to iterate over a directory. The iterator will have a private property called "$glob" which is the name of the stream (normally, this would be glob:_yourpath).

The GlobIterator is only available on systems that have glob() functionality. Some old systems like SunOS do not have this functionality. On those systems, GlobIterator is not available, yet it will still show up when calling spl_classes(). See the spl_classes() function in the miscellaneous chapter for more information about this.

This iterator is useful when you quickly need to iterate over a filtered list of files inside a directory and is preferred over a "DirectoryIterator + RegexIterator" for filtering the correct filenames.

public int GlobIterator::count (void)

This method will return the number of items that the iterator has stored. Since this iterator implements the "countable" interface, it means we can use either `$iterator->count` or `count($iterator)`.

Example

This example will return all items inside the current directory that end with the ".php" extension.

```
$it = new GlobIterator("*.php");
foreach ($it as $item) {
   print $item . PHP_EOL;
}
```

InfiniteIterator

Some things should never end. And by implementing the `InfiniteIterator` it doesn't have to. This iterator is a very simple one: the `next()` method will always return true and automatically `rewind()` when the end of the implemented iterator has been reached.

This iterator is quite useful when you need to deal with ongoing lists. But make sure you have a way to break out your `foreach()` loops, since traversing them will never end otherwise. You might do this by adding a "break" statement, or even better: chaining a `LimitIterator`.

Example

This example works with an iterator that returns consecutively the elements A,B,C,D,E. However, we want to have 25 of these items, so insert an InfiniteIterator before we limit our range. Note that without the `LimitIterator`, it would take a very long time before the `InfiniteIterator` would finish.

```
$it = new ArrayIterator(range("A", "E"));
$it = new InfiniteIterator($it);
$it = new LimitIterator($it, 0, 25);
foreach ($it as $item) {
   print $item;
```

```
 }
 /*
  Outputs:
  ABCDEABCDEABCDEABCDEABCDE
 */
```

IteratorIterator

At the moment, there are multiple traversable classes defined in PHP. For instance: the `IteratorAggregate`, `SimpleXMLElement` and `DomNodeList`, but there are others as well. But lots of (filter) iterators only work with an iterator compatible class, since it needs to work directly with its `current()` and `key()` values for instance. An `IteratorAggregate`, but also other traversable classes, do not have these methods defined.

The `foreach()` functionality in PHP automatically detects what needs to be done, so it works perfectly with an iterator or `IteratorAggregate` or anything else that is traversable. However, user-land classes like the SPL iterators (even though they are defined inside the core), and your own extended classes cannot automatically detect this.

We could create a solution for this with the following example:

```
$it = new myIterator();
if ($it instanceof IteratorAggregate) {
  $it = $it->getIterator();
}
$it = new LimitIterator($it, 5, 10);
```

But this would clutter our code everywhere. And whenever a new traversable class gets implemented in PHP, we must change our code on many places to make sure it works for that new traversable class too. So this is not the correct way.

The `IteratorIterator` turns anything that is traversable into a standard iterator, which means that the following code will always work, and will stay functioning in the future as well:

```
$it = new myIterator(); // Anything that is traversable.
$it = new IteratorIterator($it);
$it = new LimitIterator($it, 5, 10);
```

The `IteratorIterator` can create an iterator out from anything that has implemented traversable. This means that the output of the `IteratorIterator` is always an iterator which can be used for further chaining.

Always be careful when "converting" a traversable into an iterator. They are not the same thing. As I said before, iterator and IteratorAggregate are easily casted, but that does not apply to all traversable classes currently present or in the future. There is always a reason why an object would be based on the traversable interface instead of the iterator interface.

LimitIterator

A `LimitIterator` is a way to limit the elements from an iterator. If you are familiar with database programming, you can see this as defining an `OFFSET` and a `LIMIT` to your results. The offset decides where in the iterator we should start, and the limit tells us how many elements we need.

It is no problem to have a larger `LIMIT` than there are actual elements. It will stop when it hits the end of the iterator. But specifying a lower offset than 0 will result in the `LimitIterator` throwing an `OutOfRangeException`.

Example

This example will limit an iterator which contains every letter of the alphabet to only 5 letters starting from the fifth letter. As a result, it will return the letters 'E' to 'I'.

```
$it = new ArrayIterator(range('A', 'Z'));
$it = new LimitIterator($it, 4, 5);
print_r(iterator_to_array($it));
```

Using a larger limit does not matter:

```
$it = new ArrayIterator(range('A', 'Z'));
$it = new LimitIterator($it, 4, 100);
print_r(iterator_to_array($it));
```

MultipleIterator

The `MultipleIterator` can be used to iterate over multiple iterators at the same time. This differs from the `AppendIterator` since that iterator returns values in series, while this iterator returns values in parallel. When you have attached 10 iterators to the `MultipleIterator`, it will by default return an array with 10 values (each value is a value from each iterator).

public void attachIterator (Iterator $iterator [, string $infos])

The `attachIterator()` allows you to add a new iterator to the list.

Internally, these iterators are stored inside an `SplObjectStorage` class. With the `$info` parameter you can optionally add a key. This method will throw an exception when you add an iterator with the same key.

Because `SplObjectStorage` does not allow you to add the same iterator twice, you also cannot add the same iterator twice to the `MultipleIterator`. However, it will not result in an exception if you try.

Note that when adding a new iterator DURING the actual iterating of the `MultipleIterator`, it will start that iterator from the start. The `current()` values from the internal iterators will get "skewed". Also note that when adding iterators during our `foreach()` loop, we cannot actually fetch the first item from that iterator. So unless you really know what you are doing, it's not advisable to attach new iterators during the iterating loop.

public void containsIterator (Iterator $iterator)

This will return a Boolean whether or not an iterator is already attached to the `MultipleIterator`. When so, it will return `true`, otherwise, a `false` is returned.

public void countIterators (void)

This method will return the number of iterators that are currently added to the `MultipleIterator`.

Example

This example will in parallel return elements from the three iterators. Because we use the default flags in our `MultipleIterator`, it will only return elements when ALL the internal iterators return valid elements. This means that the last three items from `$it3` will not be returned.

```
$it1 = new ArrayIterator(
    array("foo", "bar", "baz"));
$it2 = new ArrayIterator(
    array("alpha", "beta", "gamma"));
$it3 = new ArrayIterator(
    array("php", "python", "perl", "java", "c", "pascal"));

$it = new MultipleIterator();
$it->attachIterator($it1);
$it->attachIterator($it2);
$it->attachIterator($it3);

foreach ($it as $item) {
    print_r($item);
}
```

NoRewindIterator

The `NoRewindIterator` is a simple iterator that cannot be rewound by the `rewind()` method. It's useful for iterators that are one-way only: you can read each element only once.

Because the iterator is not rewindable, it means it's a one-time iterator only. It might be useful to have such an iterator to make sure data that is used inside the iterator cannot be used multiple times: For instance, an iterator that generates (one-time) passwords, or any other data that should be only used once.

Example

This example will only allow you to use the iterator once.

```
$it = new ArrayIterator(array("foo", "bar", "baz"));
$it = new NoRewindIterator($it);
foreach ($it as $item) {
   print $item . PHP_EOL;
}
foreach ($it as $item) {
   print $item . PHP_EOL;
}
```

ParentIterator

The `ParentIterator` is a quick `RecursiveFilterIterator` that only returns the items that have children. It does not however, return those children so it cannot detect multi-dimensional entries. For instance, the following does not work as expected:

```
$it = new RecursiveArrayIterator(
   array("foo", array("bar", array("foo"))));
$it = new ParentIterator($it);
foreach ($it as $v) {
   print $v . PHP_EOL;
}
```

This would return "`array()`", since the `hasChildren()` for the first item will return true. However, it does not recurse deeper into the structure.

This iterator is useful for filtering out elements that CAN be recursed.

RecursiveArrayIterator

This iterator is an `ArrayIterator` which has implemented `RecursiveIterator` interface (yes, sometimes the naming is weird; one might have expected to have named the interface "Recursivable"). It enables the possibility of recursive iterating of an array. In other words: it can iterate multi-dimensional arrays.

You have to use the `hasChildren()` and `getChildren()` methods yourself to check for deeper lying iterators. For example, the following would not work as you would expect:

> One of the biggest mistakes people make with RecursiveIterators is that by itself it does not iterate recursively. It only enables this possibility.

```
$it = new RecursiveArrayIterator(
   array("foo", "bar", array("qux", "wox"), "baz"));
foreach ($it as $v) {
   print $v . PHP_EOL;
}

/* OUTPUTS:
   foo
   bar
   Array
   baz
*/
```

The `RecursiveIteratorIterator` can be used to traverse through these multiple dimensions:

```
$it = new RecursiveArrayIterator(
   array("foo", "bar", array("qux", "wox"), "baz"));
$it = new RecursiveIteratorIterator($it);
foreach ($it as $v) {
   print $it->getDepth() . " " . $v . PHP_EOL;
}

/* OUTPUTS:
   0 foo
   0 bar
   1 qux
   1 wox
   0 baz
*/
```

Iterating over objects

The `RecursiveArrayIterator` can recursively iterate over arrays and objects. When encountering an object, it will iterate over all (public) properties. However, you can set an undocumented flag through the `setFlags()` method to control this behavior: `CHILD_ARRAYS_ONLY`. When this flag is set, it will only recurse over arrays and when encountering an object, it will cast this object to a string before returning. The object itself does not get iterated.

```php
class A {
    var $foo = "A foo";
    var $bar = "A bar";

    function __toString() {
        return "class A";
    }
}

$obj = new A;

$it = new RecursiveArrayIterator(
    array("foo", array("bar", $obj), $obj));
$it->setFlags($it->getFlags() |
                RecursiveArrayIterator::CHILD_ARRAYS_ONLY);
$it = new RecursiveIteratorIterator($it);
foreach ($it as $v) {
    print $it->getDepth() . " " . $v . PHP_EOL;
}
```

This will output:

```
0 foo
1 bar
1 class A
0 class A
```

while without the `setFlags()` line, it will result in:

```
0 foo
1 bar
2 A foo
2 A bar
1 A foo
1 A bar
```

Iterators

RecursiveCachingIterator

This iterator is the recursive version of the standard `CachingIterator`. All the standard functionality that is provided by the default `CachingIterator` is applicable for this iterator as well. The only difference is the implementation of the `hasChildren()` and `getChildren()` methods, plus the fact that it will "cache" the next value, even if this is inside a child.

Flags

By default this iterator enables the `CATCH_GET_CHILD` flag. When an exception occurs during the `getChildren()` method, it will ignore this exception and continue with fetching the next element. You can unset it through either the constructor or the `setFlags()` method.

Example

This example will iterate over a recursive array, and return the cached results.

```
$it = new RecursiveArrayIterator(
    array("a", "b", "c",
        array("d", "e", array("f"), "g"), "h"));
$it = new RecursiveCachingIterator($it,
    RecursiveCachingIterator::FULL_CACHE);
$it = new RecursiveIteratorIterator($it);
foreach ($it as $v) { }

print_r($it->getCache());

/*
 Array
 (
    [0] => a
    [1] => b
    [2] => c
    [3] => Array
        (
            [0] => d
            [1] => e
            [2] => Array
                (
                    [0] => f
                )

            [3] => g
        )
    [4] => h
 )
*/
```

Iterators

RecursiveCallbackFilterIterator

This iterator enables recursive iteration over a callback filter. All functionality is equal to that of the normal `CallbackFilterIterator`. Note that your callback function must also return true when the item has children. Otherwise it will not be iterated recursively.

Example

This example will iterate recursively over a directory and return the elements (directory entries) that are 1024 bytes or less. It must also return any directories as well, otherwise only files in the top directory will be returned. Note that we also have to provide the `RecursiveIteratorIterator` to enable traveling over the children.

```php
$it = new RecursiveDirectoryIterator("/my/dir");
$it = new RecursiveCallbackFilterIterator($it,
    function($value, $key, $item) {
        if ($value->isDir ()) {
            return true;
        }
        return ($value->getSize() < 1024);
    }
);

$it = new RecursiveIteratorIterator($it);
foreach ($it as $item) {
    print $item->getSize() . " "
        . $item->getPathName() . PHP_EOL;
}
```

RecursiveDirectoryIterator

Even though the name suggests it, this iterator is not the counterpart of the `DirectoryIterator`. Since PHP 5.3, this class actually extends the `FilesystemIterator` to achieve a little bit more functionality when dealing with key and current values.

> Don't use the CURRENT_AS_PATHNAME flag. This breaks the RecursiveDirectoryIterator's functionality of detecting children since it expects that the current() returns an object, not a string.

You can set the
`RecursiveDirectoryIterator::FOLLOW_SYMLINKS` flag which
also iterates over directories that are sym-linked. Normal behavior is that
these directories are skipped.

public string getSubPathname (void)

Returns the path and filename of the current entry that is being iterated.
Note that this must be fetched from the iterator, not the iterating value.

bool hasChildren ([bool $allow_links])

It doesn't look like the `$allow_links` parameter is actually used. It will
always be called with a `NULL` value.

Example

This example will recursively iterate over a directory tree and count the
number of bytes all files and directories take up.

```
$it = new RecursiveDirectoryIterator("/my/dir");
$it = new RecursiveIteratorIterator($it);

$size = 0;
foreach ($it as $item) {
    $size += $it->getSize();
}

print "Estimated size of the directory in bytes: "
    . $size . PHP_EOL;
```

RecursiveFilterIterator

This iterator is the recursive equivalent of the
standard abstract `FilterIterator`. Extend
this class if you need to create a filter that
must be capable of recursive filtering through
the `hasChildren()` and `getChildren()`
methods.

> The accept() method must always return true for items that contains children, otherwise they will not be iterated!

Example

This example will filter recursively all files that are younger than 3600 seconds (one hour).

```
class MyRecFilterIterator extends RecursiveFilterIterator {
    public function accept() {
        if ($this->current()->isDir()) {
            return true;
        }

        $delta_time = time() - $this->current()->getMTime();
        return ($delta_time < 3600);
    }
}

$it = new RecursiveDirectoryIterator("/my/dir");
$it = new MyRecFilterIterator($it);
$it = new RecursiveIteratorIterator($it);
foreach ($it as $item) {
    print $item->getPathName() . PHP_EOL;
}
```

RecursiveIteratorIterator

The purpose of the RecursiveIteratorIterator is to turn any RecursiveIterator into a "plain" iterator so you can traverse it linearly even though the data is recursive (like a directory containing subdirectories). The RecursiveIteratorIterator is the equivalent of the IteratorIterator but it differs in what to accept. Even though the manual suggests that it accepts anything that implements the Traversable interface, this is not completely true. The RecursiveIteratorIterator only accepts either a RecursiveIterator OR an IteratorAggregate. The IteratorAggregate can only be accepted by the RecursiveIteratorIterator when it returns a RecursiveIterator through its getIterator() method. Other traversable objects will not be accepted by the RecursiveIteratorIterator.

```
class A implements IteratorAggregate {
   public function getIterator() {
      return new RecursiveArrayIterator(array("B"));
   }
}

// This will be accepted because it's an RecursiveIterator
$it = new RecursiveArrayIterator(array("a"));
$it = new RecursiveIteratorIterator($it,
   RecursiveIteratorIterator::LEAVES_ONLY);
print_r (iterator_to_array($it));

// This will be accepted as it returns an RecursiveIterator
$it = new A();
$it = new RecursiveIteratorIterator($it,
   RecursiveIteratorIterator::LEAVES_ONLY);
print_r (iterator_to_array($it));
```

When our IteratorAggregate does not return a
RecursiveIterator, it will result in
RecursiveIteratorIterator throwing an
InvalidArgumentException.

```
class B implements IteratorAggregate {
   public function getIterator() {
      // Not a recursive iterator
      return new ArrayIterator(array("B"));
   }
}

// This will not be accepted because
// it doesn't return a RecursiveIterator
$it = new B();
$it = new RecursiveIteratorIterator($it,
   RecursiveIteratorIterator::LEAVES_ONLY);
print_r (iterator_to_array($it));
```

Flags

This iterator accepts a few flags which can be set by the constructor only.
There is no setFlags() method in this iterator.

- LEAVES_ONLY - When an item has children, it will only return those children, but not the item itself. In case of iterating a directory recursively, this means that it will only return the files, not the directory entries.

- CHILD_FIRST - This will return the children of an item before the actual item. In case of directory iteration, it will return first the files inside the directory, and then the actual directory.

- SELF_FIRST - This is the opposite of CHILD_FIRST. It will first return the element, and then it will iterate its children.

Controlling the Depth of the Iteration

The RecursiveIteratorIterator has a nice feature that allows you to control the depth of recursion. By default, it will recurse as deep as needed, but with the setMaxDepth() method, you can control how deep the recursion should be. By specifying a maximum depth of 0, it will effectively turn the RecursiveIterator into a normal non-recursive iterator.

```
$it = new RecursiveArrayIterator(
    array("a", array("b", array("c", array("d")))));
$it = new RecursiveIteratorIterator($it);
$it->setMaxDepth(1);
foreach ($it as $v) {
    print $it->getDepth() . " " . $v . PHP_EOL;
}

/**
Returns:
0 a
1 b
*/
```

Iteration Hooks

This iterator supports "hooks". These are functions that are called when certain actions take place. Currently, the following functions-hooks are defined:

- beginChildren - Called before the iterator will iterate children of an element.

- `beginIteration` - Called at the start of the iteration.
- `endChildren` - Called when the iterator has iterated all children from an element.
- `endIteration` - Called when the iterator has finished.
- `nextElement` - Called AFTER the iterator has called `next()`.

All functions are defined as empty functions and can be overridden by your own functionality. Note that these functions are called automatically so you don't have to.

```php
class MyReItIt extends RecursiveIteratorIterator {
    function endChildren() {
        print "EC" . PHP_EOL;
    }
    function endIteration() {
        print "EI" . PHP_EOL;
    }

    public function beginIteration() {
        print "BI" . PHP_EOL;
    }

    public function beginChildren() {
        print "BC" . PHP_EOL;
    }
}

$it = new RecursiveArrayIterator(
    array("a", array("b", "c"), "d"));
$it = new MyReItIt($it);
foreach ($it as $v) {
    print $it->getDepth() . " " . $v . PHP_EOL;
}

/**
Outputs:
  BI
  0 a
  BC
  1 b
  1 c
  EC
  0 d
  EI
**/
```

By implementing these hooks, you have a more fine-grained control during the iteration process. Every single event (moving to a child, getting back from a child, going to the next element, etc.) can be hooked. Providing you with possibilities that otherwise would have been placed inside your `foreach()` loops.

RecursiveRegexIterator

This iterator is the recursive equivalent of the `RegexIterator`. For more information about how to use this iterator, take a look at the `RegexIterator` section of this chapter.

RecursiveTreeIterator

This iterator is a really easy way to create tree-like ASCII structures. The `current()` and `key()` method will actually return the current value with a prefix and postfix (which are separately accessible through `getPrefix()` and `getPostfix()`.

With the `BYPASS_CURRENT` and `BYPASS_KEY` flags, you can control if (and where) the iterator should add the prefix and postfix. When you specify `BYPASS_CURRENT` as a flag during constructing, it will return the item without any prefix and postfix.

Currently, the getPostfix() only returns an empty string. Trees are generated through the getPrefix() part only. However, it's possible to override the getPostfix() method which will automatically be called when creating the tree.

Note that this iterator does not necessarily have to generate ASCII-only structures. Because you can define your own tree-characters, it's possible to use images or other HTML-tags in order to generate the tree as well!

By default, an ASCII tree can easily be created by the following code:

```
$arr = array(
    "foo", "bar", "baz",
    array(1,2,array(3)),
    "qux"
);
$it = new RecursiveArrayIterator($arr);
$it = new RecursiveTreeIterator($it);
foreach ($it as $item) {
    print $item . PHP_EOL;
}
```

which will output the following tree:

```
    |-foo
    |-bar
    |-baz
    |-Array
    ||-1
    ||-2
    |\-Array
    |\-3
    \-qux
```

It is possible to use your own characters for generating the tree. This can be controlled through the `setPrefixPart()` method. The iterator also defines a few constants which you can use as the `$part` argument for this method. When you specify a non-existing part number, this method will throw an `OutOfRangeException`.

```
$it->setPrefixPart($it::PREFIX_END_HAS_NEXT, "+ ");
```

Example

Here is a simple example that creates a directory tree structure. It uses the `RecursiveCallbackFilterIterator` to filter out non-directories.

```
$it = new RecursiveDirectoryIterator("/my/dir",
    RecursiveDirectoryIterator::SKIP_DOTS);
$it = new RecursiveCallbackFilterIterator($it,
    function ($item) { return $item->isDir(); });
$it = new RecursiveTreeIterator($it);
foreach ($it as $item) {
    print $item . PHP_EOL;
}
```

RegexIterator

The RegexIterator is a FilterIterator that filters based on a regular expression functionality. It's a very common way to filter elements like file names or anything that is based on strings.

Even though the iterator looks very simple, it has many options which all can be set separately. The most important thing to remember is that the `RegexIterator` can work in different modes. Each mode corresponds to a different "preg" function. For instance, it's possible to use preg_split() functionality, or even preg_replace().

If you find yourself in a situation where the standard RegexIterator doesn't work the way you like to, and think about creating your own RegexIterator, take a look at these other modes. Chances are that you will find that it is already possible by changing the mode.

public int RegexIterator::setFlags (int $flags)

With this method you can set the flags that the iterator will use for parsing. There is currently only one flag that can be set, which is the RegexIterator::USE_KEY. Normally when filtering, the accept() method will cast the `current()` value to a string first, before the actual regular expression filtering takes place. If you specify the RegexIterator::USE_KEY, it will match the regular expression against the value of the key instead.

public int RegexIterator::setPregFlags (int $preg_flags)

Every mode that you can set with setMode() does have a specific set of flags: for instance, when you have set the GET_MATCH mode, you can specify the PREG_OFFSET_CAPTURE so you also capture the offset of the found match. Every mode has its own set of flags which can be found at the corresponding function in the PHP manual: http://php.net/ref.pcre.php.

public string RegexIterator::getRegex (void)

This method will return the regular expression that is currently used for filtering.

public int RegexIterator::setMode (int $mode)

This method sets the mode which the iterator will use. There are five different modes in which the iterator can parse regular expressions:

- MATCH - Returns the complete value when the regular expression matches. This is the default behavior when no flags are given.

- GET_MATCH - Returns an array with the match for the current entry. For instance, when you match the regular expression "bar(\d)" against the text "bar3", it will return an array with two items: bar3 and 3. This is identical behavior as the preg_match() function would return.

- ALL_MATCHES - Returns all matches for the current entry. When you match the regex "bar(\d)" against the text "bar3 bar5 bar6", it will return an array with two items, each with 3 items: bar3, bar5, bar6 and 3, 5, 6. Note that this mode also returns an array with empty values for every item that does not match. This is identical behavior as the preg_match_all() function.

- REPLACE - Matches and replaces the current entry. See the example below for an example of its usage.

- SPLIT - Returns an array with all items which are split by the regular expression. Its behavior is identical to preg_split(). It will return only items that can be split.

    The REPLACE mode is not fully implemented. Don't count on its usage to stay the way it is implemented now. If you need to use this mode, I would suggest you extend the RegexIterator and customize the accept() method.

Examples

This example will filter the current directory for filenames that end with the .PHP extension.

```
$it = new DirectoryIterator(".");
$it = new RegexIterator($it, "/.php$/i");
foreach ($it as $item) {
   print $item->getFileName() . PHP_EOL;
}
```

This example will use the REPLACE flag. It will replace all matching values with a string that is set by the "replacement" property of the iterator.

```
$it = new ArrayIterator(
    array('foo', 'bar bar baz', 'baz3 baz5', 'qux', 'BAR'));
$it = new RegexIterator($it, "/ba.?/i",
    RegexIterator::REPLACE);
$it->replacement = "foo";

print_r(iterator_to_array($it));
```

This example will iterate over the array and return per iteration an array of the split values. Each value itself is an array with both the value and the offset, since we are capturing this too. You can see the usage of the preg flags to send additional flags to the preg_split functionality.

```
$it = new ArrayIterator(array('foo bar', 'bar bar baz',
    'bar1 baz2', 'qux', 'BAR'));
$it = new RegexIterator($it, "/ /", RegexIterator::SPLIT);
$it->setPregFlags(
    PREG_SPLIT_NO_EMPTY | PREG_SPLIT_OFFSET_CAPTURE);

foreach ($it as $item) {
    print "This item has got " . count($item)
        . " values that have been split: " . PHP_EOL;
    foreach ($item as $value) {
        print "   " . $value[0] . " is found at offset "
            . $value[1] . PHP_EOL;
    }
}
```

SimpleXMLIterator

The SimpleXMLIterator will iterate over all the nodes from a SimpleXML element. This iterator extends the SimpleXMLElement class, and implements Countable and Iterator and RecursiveIterator. This means that elements can be counted (through $iterator->count() or count($iterator)) and it can be used for recursive iteration. For more information about SimpleXML and SimpleXMLElement, please look at the documentation at http://php.net/book.simplexml.php.

Example

```
$str = <<< XML
<?xml version="1.0" encoding="ISO8859-1" ?>
<basket>
    <article>
        <id>12345</id>
        <description>Red Stapler</description>
        <price cur="eur">10.99</price>
        <count>5</count>
    </article>
    <article>
        <id>1241</id>
        <description>printer</description>
        <price cur="eur">141.52</price>
        <count>1</count>
        <accessories>
            <article>
                <id>141</id>
                <description>Paper</description>
                <price cur="eur">3.99</price>
                <count>1</count>
            </article>
            <article>
                <id>142</id>
                <description>Ink - black</description>
                <price cur="eur">13.99</price>
                <count>1</count>
            </article>
        </accessories>
    </article>
</basket>
XML;
$it = new SimpleXMLIterator($str);
$it = new RecursiveIteratorIterator($it);
foreach ($it as $key => $item) {
    print "ITEM " . $it->getDepth() . ": " . $key .
      "=" . $item . PHP_EOL;
}
```

Iterators

Chapter 5

Interfaces

SPL defines a set of interfaces that you can implement in our own classes. Even though the set is relatively small, the interfaces themselves are very powerful. They are used for implementing functionality on mostly iterators, but you can also use most of these interfaces for your non-iterator classes if needed.

This chapter does not only describe the SPL interfaces, but also some non-SPL interfaces since they are used in the SPL as well. This set of interfaces can be found online at http://php.net/reserved.interfaces.php.

What Are Interfaces?

Before we start on the definition of the interfaces, first a quick recap on what interfaces are. Interfaces can be best seen as a contract on what a class needs to define for functionality. This would mean that you can always be sure that a class has implemented certain methods when it has implemented that interface.

An interface by itself can only consist of method definitions but no properties or method bodies. This makes interfaces a bit different than abstract classes where you can actually implement properties and methods.

Using interfaces makes it easier for us to define objects and control objects with the help of type hinting.

```
function getCount($obj) {
   if (! is_object($obj)) {
      throw new \InvalidArgumentException(
         "The argument is not an object");
   }
   if (! method_exists($obj, "count")) {
      throw new \BadMethodCallException(
         "This object does not have a count() method"
      );
   }
   return $obj->count();
}
```

which is a lot more work than using an interface:

```
function getCount(Countable $obj) {
   return $obj->count();
}
```

As you can see, using PHP's type hinting in this case makes our code much easier to read, and less work has to be performed for error checking. In this example, the countable interface defines a count() method, so we know for sure that the object passed to getCount() will always have the count() method defined.

Interfaces vs. Abstracts

In essence, interfaces and abstract classes are not really that different. They both define a contract that a new class using the interface of abstract must adhere to, but an interface cannot have its own functionality while abstract classes can implement some functionality.

Interfaces

One of the most common rules to define whether something should be an abstract class or an interface is the answer to the question: do we need to extend it, or should a class implement it? In other words: does a class that is derived from our class have a "HAS-A" or an "IS-A" relation?

When an object has an "IS-A" relation, it means it basically is an extension from the base class. Therefore the base class should be an abstract class. For example: a "car" class is a vehicle, so defining the "vehicle" as an abstract class makes more sense than defining an interface called "vehicle".

However, a vehicle could be either a vehicle that can be used on land, at/under water and in the air, or even space. So we can create different interfaces depending on their use:

```
interface flying {
   function takeoff() { };
   function land() { };
}
```

or maybe vehicles that can be used underwater:

```
interface submersible {
   function dive() { };
   function surface() { };
   function periscopeUp() { };
   function periscopeDown() { };
}
```

This interface defines methods that must be implemented for a vehicle that can be submersible. Of course, we need to create functionality that makes our vehicle dive and surface back again. And we could decide that a submersible vehicle always has periscope-functionality.

Suppose you want to create submarine classes. You probably want to create an abstract class called submarine that implements submersible. Here you would decide how a global submarine would dive, surface and how to move the periscope. From that abstract class you could create different types of submarines. So a certain type of submarine "is a" submarine, and the submarine "is a" vehicle and "has" submersible properties.

But since our vehicle could very well be a spaceship, let's provide some capabilities for future use:

```
interface warpSpeed {
    function ejectWarpCore();
    function engage($warpSpeed);
}

class NCC1701 extends vehicle implements WarpSpeed {
    // This "vehicle" has a warp core
    protected $warpcore = true;

    function ejectWarpCore() {
        $this->warpcore = false;
    }

    function engage($warpSpeed) {
        if (! $this->warpcore) {
            throw new \DomainException(
                "We cannot go to warp speed when the "
                . "warp core has been ejected"
            );
        }
        if ($warpSpeed >= 10) {
            throw new \OutOfRangeException(
                "Impossible to go that fast! "
                . "I cannot change the law of physics!"
            );
        }
        $this->warpSpeed = $warpSpeed;
    }
}
```

Another big advantage of interfaces is that you can implement multiple interfaces on one object.

Interfaces

```
class KlingonBirdOfPrey extends vehicle
      implements Cloakable, WarpSpeed {
   ...
}
```

So now a `KlingonBirdOfPrey` is still a vehicle, capable of warp speed AND it has cloaking capabilities to hide for other spaceships as well.

Because we have created separate interfaces instead of an abstract `cloakableShip` class, it's now possible to add cloaking to different (non-spaceship) objects as well:

```
class bicycle extends vehicle implements Cloakable {
   ...
}
```

How cool would it be to have a bicycle that nobody is able to see! You would never have to lock your bike anymore (but if you forget where you parked it, you probably never will find it again).

Why Not Multiple Inheritance?

Why is it that PHP will let you implement multiple interfaces but not multiple (abstract) classes? The answer can be best described by the following scenario. The reason is a bit technical: but suppose you have a class C that could extend both class A and class B:

```
class A {
   function foo {
      print "A Foo";
   }
}
class B {
   function foo {
      print "B Foo";
   }
}
class C {
   function foo {
      print "C Foo";
```

```
    }
  }
  class D extends B, C {
  }
  $obj = new D;
  $obj->foo();      // What to print!?
```

What is it that $obj->foo() should print? "B Foo" or "C Foo"?

It will be even worse when both class B and class C extend a class A. In that case, class D needs to incorporate duplicate functionality from class A through both class B and C which can lead to all kinds of internal ambiguity. Because of the diamond-like shaped form these classes make, this is often referred as the diamond problem.

This problem does not happen when dealing with multiple interfaces: the methods from the interfaces must be defined by the class that implements the interface (or a parent class). If there are multiple interfaces defining the same function, it will return an error.

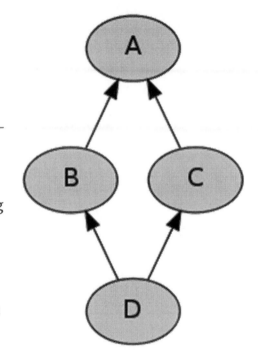

Figure 5.1

That is the reason why many object-oriented languages, including PHP only make use of single inheritance and multi interfaces.

It's not something you have to worry about, but at least you know there is actually a valid reason why.

PHP-defined vs. User-defined Interfaces

Some interfaces that are defined by PHP itself act a little different than user-defined interfaces. They can provide extra functionality on certain occasions. For instance, when you implement the `Countable` interface, it will change the behavior of the `count()` function in PHP. Instead of counting the object (which would always result in "1", since there is only one object to count), it will call the object's `count()` method. By "hooking" interfaces into the PHP core, it allows us to achieve functionality that otherwise would not be possible.

This is only possible by interfaces defined by PHP itself, since they are written in C (the language in which PHP itself is written). It is not possible for you to create this kind of functionality, unless you implement them as PHP extensions or directly in the PHP core.

Non-SPL Interfaces

Before talking about the SPL interfaces, we need to discuss some non-SPL interfaces first. Many of these interfaces are used by SPL heavily and in fact, the most common use of the SPL (the iterators) are classes based on implementations of these interfaces. So understanding these interfaces means understanding the SPL interfaces.

Even though they are considered as non-SPL interfaces, some of them actually were born during the creation of the SPL. Because of their generic functionality, they are designated as such so other extensions in PHP could use them even without enabling the SPL extension implicitly (remember that the SPL wasn't always part of the core in its infant years).

These non-SPL interfaces can be found at http://php.net/reserved.interfaces.php.

> PHP implements the traversable interface in many places besides inside the Iterator and IteratorAggregate. For instance: SimpleXMLElement, DomNodeList and even PDOStatement implement this interface.

Traversable

The Traversable interface makes an object into a traversable object through `foreach()`. Normally, when you loop over an object with `foreach()`, it will return all (public) properties of that object, but when traversable is implemented, this functionality changes so you can define which keys and values are returned.

However, the Traversable interface is a strange interface. It is not possible to implement this interface directly yourself, so only PHP extensions and the PHP core can create classes or interfaces that implement Traversable. If you attempt to implement it, PHP will throw an exception.

For actual implementation you must use either the `Iterator` or `IteratorAggregate` interfaces.

The reason that the `Traversable` interface actually exists is probably due to the fact that it's a really simple way of creating iteratable objects that wish to hide their iteration methods. For instance, the `DatePeriod` class which returns a number of `DateTime` objects between two dates on a certain interval, actually implements `Traversable` as an interface so you can use it for iteration, and so it does not need to implement the interfaces for iteration (`current()`, `key()`, `next()`, `rewind()`, etc..). And although this is only reserved for internal PHP objects, there is still debate on whether or not this is good practice.

Detecting Traversable Elements

Even though you cannot implement traversable yourself, it's useful for detecting if an object is traversable.

```
if ($object instanceof Traversable) {
    echo 'This object has implemented the traversable
    interface' . PHP_EOL;
}
```

Do not try to check if an object is traversable by checking for `Iterator` or `IteratorAggregate` directly, but use the `Traversable` interface instead. By doing this, you can even detect future traversable interfaces that might be added to PHP. However, there is always a reason why the programmer who designed the object opted for using the `Traversable` interface instead of the `Iterator` interface. So always be careful with these traversable implementations.

Iterator

Probably the most important interface of the SPL isn't actually part of the SPL itself. The "Iterator" interface can be used to make objects traversable by `foreach()`. Even though technically this could be achieved with the "Traversable" interface, we cannot as PHP developers implement that interface directly. We must implement the `Iterator` (or `IteratorAggregate`) interface instead.

Traversing an object is already possible without implementing the iterator interface. When passing a "normal" object to `foreach()`, it will iterate over its (public) properties:

```php
class foo {
    public $prop1 = "a";
    public $prop2 = "b";
    private $prop3 = "c";
}
$obj = new foo();
foreach ($obj as $key => $value) {
    print "K: ".$key." V ".$value . PHP_EOL;
}
```

this will result in:

```
K: prop1 V a
K: prop2 V b
```

With the help of the `Iterator` interface, the object itself can decide what to return as the key and value pairs. The `iterator` interface itself defines a small set of methods that needs to be implemented:

- abstract public mixed current (void)

- abstract public scalar key (void)
- abstract public void next (void)
- abstract public void rewind (void)
- abstract public boolean valid (void)

Whenever `foreach()` detects an object that is traversable, it will call these methods (except when it detects an `IteratorAggregate`, see that section for more information). Note that just defining these methods is not enough, you MUST implement the `Iterator` interface, otherwise `foreach()` will not call these methods!

The following code snippets are similar:

```
$obj->rewind();
while ($obj->valid()) {
    $key = $obj->key();
    $val = $obj->current();
    // Do something with $key and $val
    $obj->next();
}
```

versus:

```
foreach ($obj as $key => $value) {
    // Do something with $key and $val
}
```

As stated before, the iterator functionality ONLY works with `foreach()`. You cannot use the standard `current()`, `key()`, `rewind()` methods with iterators:

```
$object = new myIterator();
print current($object); // Does not work as expected!
print $object->current(); // This does work
```

Interfaces

Methods

abstract public mixed current (void)

This method will return the current value that the iterator internally points to. This value could be an internally stored value, or something that is calculated or retrieved on the fly. This allows the iterator to be much more efficient since it is not always necessary to store all information in the class prior to the iteration. The `current()` could fetch a record from the database so only one record at a time will be loaded in memory. This makes iterating large sets much more memory-efficient (although not quicker since we need to call the database for each record).

abstract public scalar key (void)

This will return the key of the value that the iterator internally points to. Some iterators do not really use keys but only return values through `current()`, however, it's always advisable to return a (unique) index as the key value even if you don't use it. It might be needed or wanted by `FilterIterator` or other users of the iterator.

abstract public void next (void)

This will result in the iterator pointing to the next internal value. The `next()` will even be called at the end of the iterator. However, before fetching the `current()`, it will check if we actually still have a valid element by calling the `valid()` method (see below).

abstract public void rewind (void)

This will result in the iterator resetting the internal pointer back to the first item. This method is called automatically prior to the `foreach()` loop so you don't need to reset the iterator manually.

abstract public boolean valid (void)

Returns true when the internal pointer points to a valid element and `current()` returns something useful. With some iterators it is possible to seek (jump) directly to a certain position. This method will check if that position is valid too.

IteratorAggregate

The IteratorAggregate is an interface needed for objects that need to have iterator capabilities, but aren't iterators by themselves. To explain this, let's define a simple "Book" iterator:

```
class Book implements Iterator {
    protected $_pages = array();
    protected $_pagePtr = 0;
    protected $_author;
    protected $_title;
    function current() {
        return $this->_pages[$this->_pagePtr];
    }
    function next() {
        return $this->_pagePtr++;
    }
    ....
}
```

Although this is a completely valid iterator, it looks a bit strange: we have a book, but the book itself is traversable. It would make more sense to actually have pages inside that book that are traversable. The main reason is simple: not everything is an iterator. Some objects have different properties, which COULD include iterators. As an example, consider a book: a book has an author, a title, a publisher, an ISBN code etc. But a book consists of pages. So when iterating a book, we basically iterate over each page.

The IteratorAggregate interface is very simple: it extends from Traversable (as does the Iterator) and only has one abstract method: getIterator(). When foreach() detects an IteratorAggregate, it will not call directly the current(), next(), etc. functionality from the object, but it will call the getIterator(). That method should return the iterator that will be used by foreach().

```
class book implements IteratorAggregate {
    protected $_pages = array();
    protected $_author;
    protected $_title;
    function getIterator() {
        return new ArrayIterator($this->_pages);
    }
}
```

Now we have removed all the iterator code from our book class but we are still able to use the $book inside a foreach() method:

```
$book = new Book();
foreach ($book as $page) {
    // Do something with each page
}
```

This makes our objects more clear and concise. Our book class does only what needs to be done and lets another class deal with iterating (in this case, an ArrayIterator). Another advantage to using the IteratorAggregate is that you can still use the object as an iterator when needed. So we can still use our book for iterating.

foreach() automatically detects what kind of traversable object you are passing. When you pass an IteratorAggregate, it will automatically iterate over the iterator that is returned by the getIterator() method.

ArrayAccess

The ArrayAccess interface makes it possible to access your object through PHP's array notation []. Note that this interface doesn't turn your object into an actual array though. Standard array functionality like most array_* functions and functions like count() will not work even when you have implemented the ArrayAccess interface. However, there are other interfaces you can implement to "emulate" arrays even more (for instance, the Countable and SeekableIterator interface).

Implementing this interface makes it easier for users to use a specific class as if it were an actual array. For instance, a shopping cart class could benefit from this interface so you could use "`$cart[] = $article`", to add another article to the cart. This interface could also be provided by other methods like "`$cart->add($article)`" so in the end it's a matter of taste. However, implementing the `ArrayAccess` can sometimes makes it easier to drop-in classes where originally arrays have been used.

Methods

abstract public boolean offsetExists (mixed $offset)

When you call `isset()` or `empty()` on an object that has `ArrayAccess` implemented, it will automatically call this method. You should return a Boolean `true` or `false` depending on existence of the element. Note that `empty()` also calls `offsetGet()` to check for an empty element as well.

abstract public mixed offsetGet (mixed $offset)

This method will retrieve the element indexed by `$offset` from your object.

abstract public void offsetSet (mixed $offset , mixed $value)

This is called when you add an element to your object. Note that you can add elements either by an index or with an empty index, which results in offset being NULL:

```
$obj[] = "foo";        // calls $obj->offsetSet(null, "foo");
$obj['test'] = "foo"; // calls $obj->offsetSet("test",
                                                "foo");
$obj[5] = "foo";       // calls $obj->offsetSet(5, "foo");
```

abstract public void offsetUnset (mixed $offset)

This method is used when you call `unset()` on an item. Normally you would unset the item from your object. It is your own responsibility to check if `$offset` falls inside the range of your object and that the element exists.

Example

This example is a simple `ArrayAccess` implementation that converts and stores all values as uppercase values.

```
class Foo implements ArrayAccess {
   protected $_arr = array();

   function offsetGet($pos) {
      return isset($this->_arr[$pos])
            ? $this->_arr[$pos] : null;
   }
   function offsetSet($pos, $val) {
      // We convert out value to uppercase before storing
      if (is_string($val)) {
         $val = strtoupper($val);
      }

      if ($pos === null) {
         $this->_arr[] = $val;
      } else {
         $this->_arr[$pos] = $val;
      }
   }
   function offsetUnset($pos) {
      unset($this->_arr[$pos]);
   }
   function offsetExists($pos) {
      return isset($this->_arr[$pos]);
   }
}
```

Serializable

The Serializable interface is a way to create custom `__sleep()` and `__wakeup()` functionality. When an object implements serializable, it no longer will call these standard magic functions during `serialize()` and `unserialize()`, but it will call the - somewhat better named - `serialize()` and `unserialize()` methods inside the object.

This interface allows you to have better control over what will happen during serialization and unserialization of your class. For instance, maybe you want serialization to be done via JSON, XML or even your own custom binary format.

Also note that you have to take care of any functionality you like to implement. Unlike the standard ___sleep() function, the serialize() will not call ___destruct() prior to the actual serialization. If you need this functionality, you need to add it yourself.

This example shows you how serializable takes care of saving and restoring properties inside your object.

```php
class Foo implements Serializable {
    public $a = "A";
    public $b = "B";
    public $c = "C";
    public function serialize() {
        // Only property "A" and "B" are saved in JSON format
        return json_encode(array($this->a, $this->b));
    }
    public function unserialize($serialized) {
        // Restore "A" and "B"
        list($this->a, $this->b) = json_decode($serialized);
    }
    function __sleep() {
        throw new \BadMethodCallException("This method is
            never called!");
    }
    function __wakeup() {
        throw new \BadMethodCallException("This method is
            never called!");
    }
}
$foo = new Foo();
$foo->a = 'a';
$foo->b = 'foo';
$foo->c = 'bar';
$tmp = serialize($foo);
$bar = unserialize($tmp);
print $bar->a . PHP_EOL;
print $bar->b . PHP_EOL;
print $bar->c . PHP_EOL;
```

Interfaces

SPL Interfaces

Countable

The `Countable` interface makes it possible to let your object handle the output of the `count()` function. Whenever you do a `count($object)`, it will normally output the value 1, since there is one object.

When you call the `count()` function with an object that has implemented the `Countable` interface, it will automatically call the `count()` method of that object. The numeric value returned will be the value that PHP's `count()` function will also return. This way you can count on whatever it is you want to count in your object. For iterators, this usually would mean the number of elements that are available for traversing.

To implement the countable interface, you must do the following:

- add the "Countable" interface to your class implementation list
- implement the `count()` method in your class.

So you must implement the interface AND add the `count()` method to your class in order for this to work.

The next example will show you how the count interface returns the actual number of items currently inside the egg basket:

```
class basket implements countable {
   protected $_eggs;
   function __construct() {
      $this->_eggs = 0;
   }
   function addEggs($count) {
      $this->_eggs += $count;
   }
   function breakAnEgg() {
      if ($this->_eggs > 1) {
         $this->_eggs--;
      }
   }
```

```
    function count() {
        return $this->_eggs;
    }
}
$basket = new Basket();
print "Eggs in basket: " . count($basket) . PHP_EOL;
$basket->addEggs(3);
print "Eggs in basket: " . count($basket) . PHP_EOL;
$basket->breakAnEgg();
print "Eggs in basket: " . count($basket) . PHP_EOL;
```

Be careful with countable and filter iterators though. Even though your iterator implements countable, this can be ignored by any filter iterators on top of your iterator:

```
$it = new ArrayIterator(array(1, 2, 3, 4));
echo count($it) . PHP_EOL;

$it = new LimitIterator($it, 3);
echo count($it) . PHP_EOL;
```

The arrayIterator implements countable, and thus will return the correct count of 4, since there are 4 elements. However, when filtering though the limit iterator, we don't get the expected response of 3 (as we limit our arrayIterator to only 3 elements), but count() will return 1. This is because the LimitIterator does NOT implement countable, and this is the actual iterator we are counting. Instead, it will use normal count() behavior and returns 1.

OuterIterator

The OuterIterator is a simple interface that extends the iterator interface with the method getInnerIterator(). This makes this interface useful for creating "filter iterators". This is normally done by passing an iterator as an argument to the constructor and storing it internally. The getInnerIterator() can be used to return that iterator and your standard current(), key(), etc. methods will return elements based on that iterator.

There aren't many cases for programmers to implement this interface directly. Most of the time you should extend the FilterIterator instead.

Interfaces

This way, you can "chain" multiple iterators to filter out information. For instance, you start with a standard `DirectoryIterator()`, and use the `RegexFilterIterator()` to filter out items based on a regular expression. That iterator can be the input for another `FilterIterator` that, for instance, would filter out elements (files) that are smaller than a certain size, or older than a particular date, etc.

The following class creates a `FilterIterator` that filters out all elements that are consonants. Note that it would be much easier to create this by extending the `FilterIterator`, but this example shows you how the `FilterIterator` works internally.

```php
class vowelFilter implements OuterIterator {
   protected $innerIterator;
   public function __construct(Iterator $it) {
      $this->innerIterator = $it;
   }
   public function accept() {
      return (! preg_match("/[aeiou]/i", $this->current()));
   }
   public function getInnerIterator() {
      return $this->innerIterator;
   }
   public function current() {
      return $this->innerIterator->current();
   }
   public function key() {
      return $this->innerIterator->key();
   }
   public function next() {
      $this->innerIterator->next();
      $this->_fetch();
   }
   public function rewind() {
      $this->innerIterator->rewind();
      $this->_fetch();
   }
   public function valid() {
      return $this->innerIterator->valid();
   }
```

```
    protected function _fetch() {
        while ($this->innerIterator->valid()) {
            if ($this->accept()) {
                return;
            }
            $this->innerIterator->next();
        }
    }
}
$iterator = new ArrayIterator(range('a','z'));
$filteredIterator = new vowelFilter($iterator);
print_r(iterator_to_array($filteredIterator));
```

RecursiveIterator

Could an iterator by itself contain iterators? And if so, would they be iterated by a `foreach()` loop as well? The answer to the first question is yes: an iterator can return elements that by themselves are iterators, but the answer to the second question: no, by default, those elements would not be iterated.

Think of this like iterating over a standard multidimensional array. When an array contains both strings and array of strings, a standard `foreach()` loop would not display the elements of the internal arrays.

The `RecursiveIterator` interface provides the means for us to iterate recursively over iterators. The keyword here is "provides", since changing your implementation from `Iterator` to `RecursiveIterator` does not magically make it recurse your data. In

Implementing the RecursiveIterator interface does not make your iterator recursive. It makes it recursivable but you have to provide your own functionality outside the iterator to actually recursive the iterator.

Implementing the RecursiveIterator makes it possible for an iterator to become recursive, but doesn't provide that functionality out of the box.

order to make this work, you have to provide your own logic to check if an item is an iterator, and recurse it manually.

The `RecursiveIterator` implements two extra methods: `hasChildren()` and `getChildren()`. The `hasChildren()` method should return true when the current item has children (which could be iterated as well) or false when they don't. The `getChildren()` method returns an iterator for those children.

Just like the `OuterIterator`, this interface is something that you normally don't implement directly. It will be used by most of the `RecursiveIterator` iterators in the SPL.

For more information about using recursive iterators, take a look at the recursive* iterators found in the SPL Iterators chapter.

SeekableIterator

The standard iterator interface implements a `next()` method, which implies iterators can only be traversed in a sequential way forward. In order to find the 10th element, you must `rewind()` the iterator, and issue 10 `next()` calls before you have access to that element. This looks somewhat similar to fetching data through a `DoublyLinkedList` data structure.

> **Your LimitIterators will be much faster when they limit an iterator that has implemented this SeekableIterator.**

In some cases, this behavior is valid and can only be traversed sequentially; for instance, when you are dealing with streams or so-called "character devices". But suppose an iterator represents the rows from a table inside a database and you want to fetch only the last record. With the help of the countable interface, you can already use `count()` to return the number of rows inside the iterator. However, you still need to iterate through all the records in order to get the last.

The `SeekableIterator` interface gives you a `seek()` method which can be used to jump directory to the position inside your iterator. So in the case of our database rows, `seek(5)` will jump directly to the 5th record. So this makes it possible to "jump" directly to the last record in the iterator as well:

```
$dbIterator->seek($dbIterator->count()-1);
$lastRecord = $dbIterator->current();
```

`SeekableIterator` is perfect for iterators where random reads are possible (and needed).

Example

This example creates a simple iterator that implements the `SeekableIterator`. It iterates and can seek elements from the NATO alphabet. With `seek()` you can easily fetch the correct element. Note that we "convert" our position in seek from a char ('A' to 'Z') to a position in the array (0..25).

```
class natoAlphabetIterator implements SeekableIterator {
    protected $data = array(
        "alpha", "bravo", "charlie", "delta",
        "echo", "foxtrot", "gamma", "hotel",
        "india", "juliet", "kilo", "lima",
        "mike", "november", "oscar", "papa",
        "quebec", "romeo", "sierra", "tango",
        "uniform", "victor", "whiskey",
        "x-ray", "yankee", "zulu"
    );
    protected $pos = 'A';

    public function current() {
        return $this->data[$this->pos];
    }

    public function next() {
        $this->pos++;
    }
```

```php
    public function key() {
        return chr (ord('A') + $this->pos);
    }

    public function valid() {
        return isset($this->data[$this->pos]);
    }

    public function rewind() {
        $this->pos = 0;
    }

    public function seek($position) {
        if ($position < 'A' || $position > 'Z') {
            throw new \InvalidArgumentException(
                "Position should be between 'A' and 'Z'");
        }

        $this->pos = ord($position) - ord('A');
    }
}

$it = new natoAlphabetIterator();

foreach ($it as $item) {
    print $item . " ";
}

print PHP_EOL;
$it->seek('P');        print $it->current() . PHP_EOL;
$it->seek('H');        print $it->current() . PHP_EOL;
$it->seek('P');        print $it->current() . PHP_EOL;
$it->seek('R');        print $it->current() . PHP_EOL;
$it->seek('O');        print $it->current() . PHP_EOL;
$it->seek('X');        print $it->current() . PHP_EOL;
```

Design Patterns in the SPL

Design patterns are a common way to describe a problem and solution for a certain problem that arises in object oriented programming. For instance, in object-oriented programming, every class can be instantiated as many

Interfaces

times as you see fit. However, sometimes you only want to be able to instantiate a single object from a class, and let all others use that particular instance. This can be the case when you have a configuration-object, or sometimes people use them for making sure only one database-class (and thus database-connection) exists inside an application. This problem - and the solution - is described as the "singleton" pattern. So when somebody is talking about whether or not a class should be singleton, you know what they are talking about, and how to actually create that singleton.

There is a book on the market that can be considered THE book on design patterns. This book is called "Design patterns - Elements of Reusable Object-Oriented Software" and is written by four authors who are more commonly known as the "Gang of Four". This book contains a lot of practical design patterns, including the ones that PHP already has implemented.

Even if you have never heard about design patterns before now, you probably already have implemented a few without knowing. Most of these design patterns are in fact very easy to comprehend (like decorators or the observer pattern) and most of them are in fact a very logical solution to solving a problem. Especially when you are more interested in object oriented programming, take a look at these design patterns and how to implement them.

The SPL defines two interfaces that make up the observer pattern. Note, that according to the "Gang of Four", the iterator is - in fact - also a design pattern. This means that the SPL defines two standard design patterns you can use directly.

Observer Pattern

The observer pattern is a great way to let objects react on changes in other objects. Suppose you have an e-commerce system, where a "shipment" class decides which kind of shipping methods can be used for delivering an order and how much this shipment would cost. In order to calculate this, our shipment class should have information from our shopping-cart object, and probably a user object, where it can find the correct delivery address.

Interfaces

Now suppose calculation takes a long time and you therefore cache the final shipping costs inside your shipment-class. But when either the user's delivery address or something in the shopping-cart changed, the shipping costs must be recalculated.

There are multiple ways to deal with this, and one way would be to add some code inside the shopping-cart class and your user-class that directly calls the generateShippingCost() method.

```
class Cart {
    function addArticle(Article $article) {
        $this->_basket[] = $article;
        $this->getShipping()->recalculateShipping();
    }
    function removeArticle($idx) {
        unset($this->_basket[$idx]);
        $this->getShipping()->recalculateShipping();
    }
}
```

Even when you refactor this into one single recalculate() method, it would still mean we have a direct dependency between the shopping cart and the shipping class. This means we never can have a shopping-cart without having a shipping-class somewhere. This is not always what you would like.

Suppose you also want to calculate payment costs (like a 3% fee for credit card payments). It would mean we have to connect our payment class directly to our cart again.

With the observer pattern, you disconnect these objects and decide at runtime which objects get connected to what. This works by having a class act as a "subject". A subject is a class that can be "observed" by another class (called the observer). An observer class tells the subject class that it is interested in receiving notifications about the subject class. When the subject class changes something (in the case of our shopping cart class, that would probably be when it adds or removes articles), the class will notify all observers of that change. These observers can then act on those

Interfaces

changes, like recalculating the shipment and payment costs.

By implementing the observer pattern, other functionality would be much easier to implement as well. Suppose you want to display articles based on the content of your shopping cart. By adding this module as an observer to the shopping-cart it's easier to implement this as well (for instance, you want to display articles like paper and ink when somebody has added a printer to their shopping cart).

Even though it sounds like a lot of work implementing this functionality, it makes more sense to create these as interfaces instead of abstract objects. With abstract objects, you wouldn't be able to extend your classes from others, as PHP doesn't support multiple inheritances. However, with the help of traits, a new PHP5.4 feature, there might be observer functionality written that can be implemented by just using those traits inside your objects.

SplObserver and SplSubject

The observer pattern consists of two "actors": the observer and the subject. The subject is the object that will be monitored by one or more observers. When something happens in the subject class, it will notify the observer objects. The observer reacts on the changes of the subject. In our example above: the shopping cart would implement the `SplSubject` interface and the shipping-costs object and shipping and delivery class object would implement the `SplObserver` interface.

When dealing with the `SplObserver` and `SplSubject`, there is (relatively) a lot you need to implement before you can work. The most work is dealing with

Note that the observers do not really observe the subject, but the subject notifies the observers. This is a much better way of communicating because the subject knows when it has changed, however it doesn't really reflect the term "observing" exactly.

Interfaces

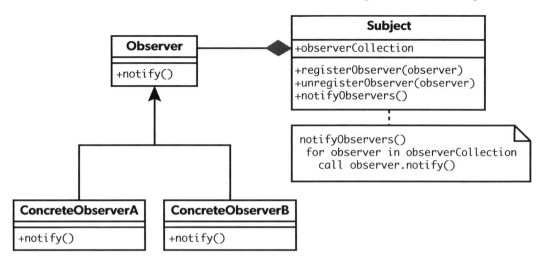

Figure 5.2

the `SplSubject`. The subject must keep a record of all the observers that are connected. Also, there must be functionality to add and remove observers and last but not least, when something happens inside the object, it must be able to notify all the observers. These functions must all be implemented, but on the whole, this is just a matter of copy and pasting the code in the example below.

The `SplObserver` are a bit easier to implement. You only need to implement an "update" method that will be called when a subject has changed.

One of the major uses of the observer pattern can be found in event-driven frameworks. The core of the event-handler, most of the time called the dispatcher, dispatches events to the observers. The observers themselves can do with the information whatever they like. They can ignore them, they can trigger a database update, they can trigger a screen refresh etc.

Example

The next example is a simple logger (the subject) where you can attach different log-sources (the observers). These sources could log the messages either to email, to file, to disk, to syslog or any other system you like to log to. The subject takes care of the actual handling of the message, to see if the message should be actually logged (in case you trigger a debug-message, but your application is configured to only log warnings or higher priority messages). This keeps the logic separated in the correct classes.

```
class logger implements SplSubject {
   protected $_observers;

   public function __construct() {
      $this->_observers = new SplObjectStorage();
   }

   public function attach (SplObserver $observer) {
      $this->_observers->attach($observer);
   }

   public function detach(SplObserver $observer) {
      $this->_observers->detach($observer);
   }

   public function notify() {
      foreach ($this->_observers as $item) {
         $item->update($this);
      }
   }

   public function getMessage() {
      return $this->_message;
   }

   public function log($message) {
      $this->_message = $message;
      $this->notify();
   }
}

class mailLog implements SplObserver {
   public function update(SplSubject $subject) {
      echo "This would be send to email: "
         . $subject->getMessage() . PHP_EOL;
   }
}
```

Interfaces

```
class fileLog implements SplObserver {
    public function update(SplSubject $subject) {
        echo "This would be send to file: "
            . $subject->getMessage() . PHP_EOL;
    }
}

// Create a new logger object
$logger = new logger();

// Create a mail logger and attach it to the logger
$maillog = new mailLog();
$logger->attach($maillog);
$logger->log("Hello world");

// Now create and attach a file logger
$filelog = new fileLog();
$logger->attach($filelog);
$logger->log("Hello again!");

// Let's remove the maillog
$logger->detach($maillog);
$logger->log("Goodbye!");
```

The Future of SPL Design Patterns

One of the goals of the SPL is standardization. When we want to implement the observer pattern, it makes our life much easier to adhere to the `SplObserver` and `SplSubject` standards to ensure interoperability with other components and/or frameworks. It allows others to easily connect their own observers, or it makes it easier for you to connect your observers to their subjects. In the end, it would mean writing lesser code, more maintainable code and more reusable code.

There is room for other design patterns to be implemented into the SPL in the future. Think about design patterns like the singleton, strategy and the visitor pattern, but also less common patterns like the flyweight or factories. However, there are currently no plans or patches that implement these patterns one way or another inside the SPL. But that should not stop you from contributing yourself!

Now that PHP has turned into an enterprise ready language, codebases are getting more complex, and implementing and using the correct design patterns is becoming an important aspect. Hopefully, the SPL will continue to grow as a generic set of design patterns, iterators and data structures to cope with the increasingly demanding programmers and applications.

Chapter 6

Exceptions

Exceptions are an object-oriented programmer's best friend. They allow you to implement a more fine-grained error control system than in traditional languages like C where most of the error control is done through function return values or external error codes. The SPL defines a wide range of exceptions that can be used in almost every scenario. By implementing these exceptions instead of using your own, it will become clearer for other programmers to see what type of exceptions your code is able to handle, and there will less ambiguity in the meaning of those exceptions.

On the SPL Exceptions

One of the major drawbacks of the SPL exceptions is that there is a lack of clear documentation on what every exception should be used for. Most exceptions are taken directly from the Java language which of course, doesn't work the same way as PHP does. This sometimes makes it unclear where and when to use certain exceptions. There is also a lot of documentation in the form of blog-posts and websites that all tell you another story. This makes using the exceptions consistently very hard for end-users. Hopefully, this chapter will take away some of the confusion about exceptions.

Hierarchy

The SPL exceptions are hierarchically structured. There are two base exceptions: the `LogicException` and the `RuntimeException`. Every other exception is based on either one of these exceptions except for the `BadMethodCallException`, which is based on the `BadFunctionCallException`. All exceptions ultimately are based on the standard `Exception` class.

None of the SPL exceptions have additional methods or properties though. They only contain the methods and properties of the standard exception class.

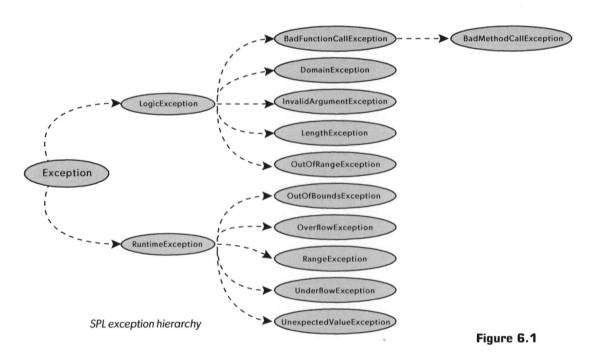

SPL exception hierarchy

Figure 6.1

Exceptions

Runtime vs. Logic Exceptions

As you can see, the exceptions are divided into 2 main groups: logic and runtime exceptions. But what is the difference between these two groups? Before we can answer this, we should take a look at some bad ways of writing code:

```
function foo($arg1, $arg2) {
   if (is_numeric($arg1) && is_string($arg2)) {
      if ($arg1 >= 0 && $arg1 <= 10) {
         if ($arg2 == "bar" || $arg2 == "baz") {
            if ($arg2 == "bar") {
               return dobar($arg1);
            } else {
               return dobaz($arg1);
            }
         } else {
            return false;
         }
      } else {
         return false;
      }
   } else {
      return false;
   }
}
```

This code is functioning, but isn't really readable or extendible. If the function returned a "false" value, we as programmer have absolutely no idea what exactly the problem was. There are many times a false is returned, so we can only debug the method in order to find out.

Furthermore, it doesn't adhere to the "failure-first" principle. This means we would check our input and do our basic setup first, and fail when something wrong has happened. From that point on, we can treat our input as being "sanitized" so we can use our input without further checking. This not only makes the code more readable, but is also less error-prone (especially when you are checking the input multiple times).

```
function foo($arg1, $arg2) {
    // Failure first
    if (! is_numeric($arg1) || ! is_string($arg2)) {
        return false;
    }
    if ($arg1 < 0 || $arg1 > 10) {
        return false;
    }
    if ($arg2 != "bar" && $arg2 != "baz") {
        return false;
    }
    // Do our business stuff from this point on.
    if ($arg2 == "bar") {
        return dobar($arg1);
    } else {
        return dobaz($arg1);
    }
}
```

This is a somewhat better refactoring of the same function. The first few blocks of code do nothing besides checking and validating our input. When everything is ok, it will continue with doing the business part of the function. You can see the difference in code: we don't need a lot of deep nesting (which normally is an indicator for 'codesmell'), and it's much clearer to see the flow of the function. But there is still the problem of not knowing what exactly went wrong afterwards, since we are still returning false everywhere.

```
function foo($arg1, $arg2) {
    // Fail first
    if (! is_numeric($arg1) || ! is_string($arg2)) {
        throw new \InvalidArgumentException(
            "The type of a parameter is incorrect");
    }
    if ($arg1 < 0 || $arg1 > 10) {
        throw new \OutOfRangeException(
            "Argument must be between 0 and 10");
    }

    if ($arg2 != "bar" && $arg2 != "baz") {
        throw new \InvalidArgumentException(
```

Exceptions

```
                "Argument must be \"bar\" or \"baz\"");
    }

    // Do our business from this point on.
    if ($arg2 == "bar") {
        if (! dobar($arg1)) {
            throw new \UnexpectedValueException(
                "dobar failed!");
        }
    } else {
        if (! dobaz($arg1)) {
            throw new \UnexpectedValueException(
                "dobaz failed!");
        }
    }
}

try {
    foo("5", "bar");
} catch (\LogicException $e) {
    print "Incorrect data: ".$e->getMessage()
        . PHP_EOL;
    exit;
} catch (\RuntimeException $e) {
    print "Something went wrong: ".$e->getMessage()
        . PHP_EOL;
    exit;
}
print "All is ok" . PHP_EOL;
```

This is yet another refactoring of the same function, but now we will be using exceptions instead of returning a Boolean `true` or `false` to indicate success or failure. As a programmer, we expect this function to ALWAYS work. When it doesn't, something unexpected has occurred and therefor an exception has occurred.

Note that because of the refactoring earlier on, we can easily distinguish now between the logic part - the part that does the checking and sanitizing of the input - and the business part, or the runtime part. As a rule of thumb: logic exceptions are thrown when dealing with user-input and can be found at the start of the function, runtime exceptions are thrown during runtime.

This allows the users of your functions to deal with the exceptions properly. As you can see in the example above, when a `LogicException` has been thrown, we know something is wrong with the user-input. We can change this by either fixing our code (for instance, we give wrong parameters), or by telling the user that he entered incorrect input.

However, runtime exceptions aren't directly fixable by the user. In our example, we have no control over the `dobar()` and `dobaz()` functions. We don't expect them to fail, so when they do, we throw a runtime exception. A good place to do this is when you are writing a record to your database (normally, this should always work).

Throwing the Correct Exception

Always make sure you use the most detailed exception that can be thrown. For instance, when you find that somebody is passing an index to an array that is outside its range, you should throw a `RangeException` instead of a `RuntimeException` or standard `Exception`. This way, it's easier for the user (or you) to detect what went wrong, and in some cases, you can even recover from it. As I've shown you in the example above, by throwing the correct exceptions, we give the caller the power to deal with exceptions the way he wants. In our case, we distinguish

> **Returning the most detailed exception results in your code being flexible to work with. Let your users decide how they want to take care of exceptions.**

between `LogicExceptions` and `RuntimeExceptions`, or maybe the caller only wants to deal with the `OutOfRangeException` (since that could be a value that is taken from user input).

However, keep in mind that exceptions are what they are: exceptions. Do not use exceptions as a standard part of your control flow, as demonstrated in the following example:

Exceptions

```
function hasKey($key) {
    if (! isset($this->_arr[$key])) {
        throw new OutOfRangeException();
    }
    return true;
}
```

The hasKey() obviously can return either a Boolean true or false. But in our case, it will only return true when the key is found, but throws an exception when the key is not found. In this case, this is the wrong way of dealing with exception. We can "expect" that when asking a question, the answer might be "no" (even though we may not like it, it is a valid response). So the fact that a key does not exist isn't an exception but expected behavior.

Consider the next example:

```
function containsValue($value) {
    if (! is_numeric($value)) {
        throw new InvalidArgumentException(
            "Argument passed is not a numeric value");
    }
    return in_array($value, $this->_arr);
}
```

In this case, our method will check if a numeric value exists in our internal array: it can return either a Boolean true or false. But since we are checking numeric values, we don't want to check against strings, arrays, objects or any other non-numerical values since that might result in unspecified behavior.

The first line in our method will check if our $value argument actually contains a numerical value, and if not, it will throw an exception. It would not be wise to either let PHP automatically cast the value to a numeric value (sometimes it can, sometimes it can't, sometimes it will cast wrong). In our case, the method cannot continue with returning a correct answer, so we throw an exception. It's up to the caller function to catch that exception and if possible correct the error (cast the value to a numeric value, let the user re-enter its input etc.).

So when dealing with SPL exceptions or any exception in general, always be aware of the condition in which you throw the error. Does something happen that interrupts the flow of your method? If so, throw an exception, otherwise don't.

SPL Exceptions

Each of the following exceptions will be accompanied by some additional information: the exception's base class, its main usage, a description and an example. Again, always try to find the best exception for your situation (instead of just catching "Exception") to make your code more solid.

BadFunctionCallException

Base class: `LogicException`

Main usage: Throw when making a call to a bad or non-existing function in your application.

A `BadFunctionCallException` is not really an exception you would use very often. Its main purpose is to catch the fact that you are calling a function directly but you are not allowed to do so. Using a `BadFunctionCallException` implies bad coding practice: you are somehow organizing and/or securing calls to functions that can be called directly anyway.

```
function func1() {
   print "This is function1" . PHP_EOL;
}

function func2() {
   print "This is function2" . PHP_EOL;
}

function callFunction($function_number) {
   if (! function_exists("func".$function_number)) {
```

Exceptions

```
        throw new BadFunctionCallException(
            "This function does not exist!");
    }
    call_user_func("func".$function_number);
}

try {
    callFunction(1);
    callFunction(2);
    callFunction(3);
} catch (BadFunctionCallException $e) {
    print "Exception has occurred: " . $e->getMessage()
        . PHP_EOL;
}
```

BadMethodCallException

Base class: BadFunctionCallException (LogicException)

Main usage: Throw when somebody calls a method that does not exist in
your class.

This method is the "object-oriented" variant of
BadFunctionCallException. Whereas using the
BadFunctionCallException is not considered a good
practice (or at least: if you need it, you are doing it wrong), the
BadMethodCallException is a good way of dealing with dynamic
method calls.

```
class myClass {
    function __call($name, $arguments) {
        $methodName = $name."Action";
        if (! method_exists($this, $methodName)) {
            throw new BadMethodCallException("
                Action $name does not exist");
        }

        return $this->$methodName($arguments);
    }

    protected function fooAction() {
```

```
        return"foo" . PHP_EOL;
    }

    protected function barAction() {
        return "bar" . PHP_EOL;
    }
}

$my = new myClass();

try {
    print $my->foo();
    print $my->bar();
    print $my->baz();
} catch (\BadMethodCallException $e) {
    print "Exception: ".$e->getMessage() . PHP_EOL;
}
```

Because the "action" methods inside our class are protected, we cannot call them from outside the class itself. The __call() method is the only way to call these action-methods. This is for instance a nice way to create a controller class for handling URL's:

```
//  Fetch the action and arguments from the URL
$arguments = explode("/", $_SERVER['PATH_INFO!']);
array_shift($arguments);
$action = array_shift($arguments);

// If no action was given, we look for the "default" action
if (empty($action)) {
    $action = "default";
}

// Now create our class and call our action (if exists)
$class = new myClass();
try {
    print $class->$action($arguments);
} catch (BadMethodCallException $e) {
    // It did not exist, so we return a 404-not found page.
    header("HTTP/1.1 404 Not found");
    print "The page you are looking for was not found: "
```

Exceptions

```
        . $e->getMessage();
   }
```

DomainException

Base class: `LogicException`

Main usage: Catch when something happens that is not conforming to your domain rules.

`DomainException` is thrown when in essence the logic is correct, but you have specific rules on how it should work. For instance, you could have a function that accepts only prime or odd numbers.

Domain exceptions should reflect the working of your domain instead of the inner workings. And because your domain differs per application (or even part of the application), the `DomainException` should be extended to reflect a more detailed exception.

Suppose you have a calendar class that allows you to insert an appointment on a certain date. However, your class does not allow you to add an appointment during the weekends, or on Christmas day.

```
class InvalidDateException extends DomainException { }
class ChristmasException extends DomainException { }

class Calendar {
   function addAppointment(DateTime $date, $appointment) {
      if ($date->format("dm") == "2512") {
         throw new ChristmasException(
            "Cannot add appointment on Christmas day");
      }

      $weekday = $date->format("N");
      if ($weekday >= 6) {
         throw new InvalidDateException(
            "Cannot add appointment in the weekend");
      }

      // Add appointment to calendar
```

```
        . . . .
    }
}

$cal = new Calendar();

// It's ok to add an appointment on Wednesday
$cal->addAppointment(new DateTime("2012-02-01 19:00"),
    "Goto PHP Usergroup");

// But we cannot add one in the weekend
$cal->addAppointment(new DateTime("2012-02-04 14:00"),
    "Scrum session");

// And we cannot go to work on Christmas day
$cal->addAppointment(new DateTime("2012-12-25 09:00"),
    "Do some work");
```

InvalidArgumentException

Base class: `LogicException`

Main usage: Throw when invalid arguments are given to methods and functions.

PHP supports type hinting. We can supply an optional type to function-arguments which are automatically checked by PHP on runtime to make sure the argument is actually of the specified type (or descendant of it).

```
function doSomething(Iterator $it) {
    ...
}
```

This will automatically throw an exception when the argument passed is not of the `Iterator` class. However, this only works with classes (interfaces) and arrays. It is not possible to type hint strings, integers, floats etc. This means we still have to check those manually. When our method does not support the given argument type, we should throw an `InvalidArgumentException`.

Exceptions

```php
function findItem(Iterator $it, $count) {
    if (! is_numeric($count)) {
        throw new InvalidArgumentException(
            "The \$count argument should be a numerical value");
    }
}
```

Another example:

If you have ever dealt with CRUD functionality (create, retrieve, update, delete), you will find that adding and updating a record is very similar on most occasions. It is because of this, a lot of CRUD systems use the same logic for both adding and updating records:

```php
<?php
function update($record) {
    return $this->_mutate("update", $record);
}
function add($record) {
    return $this->_mutate("insert", $record)
}
function _mutate($mode, $record) {
    // ... do all kind of checks to see if record is ok
    $result = false;
    if ($mode == "update") {
        $result = $database->update($record)
    } elseif ($mode == "insert") {
        $result = $database->insert($record);
    }
    return $result
}
```

The _mutate() method should only be called with either the $mode being "insert" or "update". This means a check is in order to see if we passed the correct mode:

```php
function _mutate($mode, $record) {
    if ($mode != "update" && $mode != "insert") {
        throw new InvalidArgumentException(
            "mode should be 'update' or 'insert'");
    }
    ...
}
```

Exceptions

This exception is similar to the UnexpectedValueException. However, that exception should be thrown when you receive an unexpected value from a function, not from arguments. That is why this exception extends the LogicException, and UnexpectedValueException extends the RuntimeException.

LengthException

Base class: `LogicException`

Main usage: Catch when the length of a value is too short or too long.

A `LengthException` can be thrown when you decide that the length of your data is incorrect. For instance: suppose you have a "Person" class where you can set the name of the user. Because you store this information inside a database, you decide that the maximum length for a name can be 50 characters at the most:

```
function setFullName($fullname) {
    if (! is_string($fullname)) {
        throw new InvalidArgumentException(
            "The name must be a string");
    }

    if (mb_strlen($fullname) > 50) {
        throw new LengthException(
            "The name must have a maximum of 50 characters");
    }

    $this->_fullname = $fullname;
}
```

As you can see, we throw 2 different exceptions here: the `InvalidArgumentException` when the string is not a string or a `LengthException` when the length of the string is too large.

It's up to the caller to decide how to handle this. For instance, when the length of the string is too long, it might automatically deal with shortening the name. In this case, the system can automatically correct the problem.

Exceptions

However, when no string is given, and an `InvalidArgumentException` is thrown, it cannot correct automatically. It has to ask the user again for new (and correct) input, or maybe even fail the application.

LogicException

Base class: `Exception`

Main usage: Catch a generic logical error in your program.

`LogicException` is one of the SPL base exception classes that can be used for catching generic logical errors. Always look for a better suited (logic)exception, since you should throw that particular exception instead of this one.

```
function query(SQLQuery $query) {
    if ($this->_database == null) {
        throw new LogicException(
            "You should connect to the database first!");
    }
}
```

OutOfBoundsException

Base class: `RuntimeException`

Main usage: Throw when an index falls outside the range of the array/container

This exception is commonly used to check if a value falls inside the bounds on an array (or container). It's not the same as the `RangeException` which would just check to see if a number falls inside a range (but has nothing to do with indexes) and it's not the same as `OutOfRangeException`, which is a `LogicException` to check if the user input falls inside an index boundary.

OutOfRangeException

Base class: `LogicException`

Main usage: catch exceptions where an index falls outside the range of an array.

The `OutOfRangeException` is a logic exception so it should be used for catching logical errors, not runtime ones. For that purpose, the `OutOfBoundsException` should be thrown. This exception should be used to indicate that you are requesting an index from an array (or container) that falls outside of the boundaries.

This exception is useful to throw when you are implementing the **ArrayAccess** interface in your `offsetGet()` and `offsetUnset()` methods.

```php
class Foo implements ArrayAccess {
    protected $_arr = array();

    function offsetGet($pos) {
        if (!isset($this->_arr[$pos])) {
            throw new \OutOfRangeException(
                "Incorrect offset specified");
        }
        return $this->_arr[$pos];
    }
    function offsetSet($pos, $val) {
        if (is_string($val)) {
            $val = strtoupper($val);
        }
        if ($pos === null) {
            $this->_arr[] = $val;
        } else {
            $this->_arr[$pos] = $val;
        }
    }
    function offsetUnset($pos) {
        if (!isset($this->_arr[$pos])) {
            throw new \OutOfRangeException(
                "Incorrect offset specified");
```

```
        }
        unset($this->_arr[$pos]);
    }
    function offsetExists($pos) {
        return isset($this->_arr[$pos]);
    }
}
```

OverflowException

Base class: `RuntimeException`

Main usage: When your class has reached a certain limit, but somebody is adding more data to it.

The `OverflowException` is thrown when you want to add more elements to a container (could be an object, or array, or maybe something else that could hold elements), and it's not possible to add more elements. In our example, we simulate an egg basket that has room for only 10 eggs. If we want to add an 11th egg, it would literally overflow our basket.

```
class Basket {
    protected $_eggs;

    function __construct($size) {
        $this->_size = $size;
        $this->_eggs = new SplStack();
    }

    function add($egg) {
        if (count($this->_eggs) >= $this->_size) {
            throw new OverflowException(
                "No room for more eggs inside the basket");
        }
        $this->_eggs->push($egg);
    }

    function get() {
        if (count($this->_eggs) == 0) {
            throw new UnderflowException(
                "The basket is already empty");
```

```
        }
        return $this->_eggs->pop();
    }
}

$basket = new Basket(3);
try {
    $basket->add("egg 1");
    $basket->add("egg 2");
    $basket->add("egg 3");
    $basket->add("egg 4");
} catch (\OverflowException $e) {
    print "Exception: " . $e->getMessage() . PHP_EOL;
}
```

RangeException

Base class: `RuntimeException`

Main usage: Throw this exception to indicate range errors during program execution.

It would be tempting to use this exception for checking if user input falls in a certain range. For instance: when you only want to accept numeric values between 0 and 10. But this should be done with the `OutOfRangeException`, since that exception extends the `LogicException`.

This exception however, extends the `RuntimeException`, meaning it should be used for runtime checking. Throw this exception when a value doesn't fall inside a range. For instance: you expect a `dayOfTheWeek()` method to return a number between 1 (Monday) and 7 (Sunday), but not 0, 12 or 15.

```
function isWeekendOrHoliday(DateTime $date, $hour) {
    if ($hour < 0 && $hour > 23) {
        throw new \OutOfRangeException(
            "The hour must be between 0 and 23");
    }
```

```
$dow = $date->format("N");
if ($dow <= 0 || $dow >= 8) {
    throw new \RangeException(
        "This date returns a incorrect weekday");
}
...
}
```

Do you see the difference between runtime and logic exceptions here? If there was something wrong with the data object itself, it should throw a `LogicException`. In this case, something is wrong with the `$date->format()` call, since it returns a value that falls outside the range we expect.

RuntimeException

Base class: `Exception`

Main usage: To catch a generic runtime error in your program.

The `RuntimeException` should be thrown when something unexpected is happening during the operational (runtime) part of your method. For instance: when you want to write to the database, but this results in an error, when you want to open a file, but the file isn't readable or when you are consuming an HTTP service which returns an unexpected 400 or 500 status code.

When you don't have a more specific exception to return, this exception should be thrown, but in many cases other exceptions like `UnexpectedValueException` or `OutOfBoundsException` are a better choice.

```
class DBRecord {
    protected $_database; // A database class

    function write() {
        if (! $this->_database) {
            throw new \RuntimeException(
                "There is no database connection available");
```

```
    }

    if (! $this->_database->save($this)) {
        throw new \UnexpectedValueException(
            "Cannot write record to database");
    }
    }
}

$record = new DBRecord();
$record->name = "Joshua";
$record->email = "joshua@example.org";

try {
    $record->write();
} catch (RuntimeException $e) {
    print "Error while saving record: "
        . $e->getMessage() . PHP_EOL;
}
```

UnderflowException

Base class: `RuntimeException`

Main usage: When your class can store data, but somebody is removing data when no data can be removed (most of the time, because there is no data yet stored).

When dealing with containers and structures, throwing an `UnderflowException` means you want to remove more than would be possible. For instance: when you want to pop an element from an empty stack. In such cases, an `underFlow` exception would be the correct exception to throw.

It should be noted that even the SPL itself doesn't always use the best exception: when you want to `pop()` an element from a `splDoublyLinkedList` (or extended class like `splStack` or `splQueue`), it will throw a `RuntimeException` instead of the expected `UnderflowException`.

Exceptions

```
class Basket {
   protected $_eggs;

   function __construct($size) {
      $this->_size = $size;
      $this->_eggs = new SplStack();
   }

   function add($egg) {
      if (count($this->_eggs) >= $this->_size) {
         throw new OverflowException(
             "No room for more eggs inside the basket");
      }
      $this->_eggs->push($egg);
   }

   function get() {
      if (count($this->_eggs) == 0) {
         throw new UnderflowException(
             "The basket is already empty");
      }
      return $this->_eggs->pop();
   }
}

$basket = new Basket(3);
$basket->add("egg1");
try {
   $basket->get();
   $basket->get();
   $basket->get();
} catch (\UnderflowException $e) {
   print "Exception: " . $e->getMessage() . PHP_EOL;
}
```

UnexpectedValueException

Base class: RuntimeException

Main usage: Throw when the returned value of a called method wasn't what you have expected.

Sometimes functions and methods don't always return what you are expecting. In some cases, this would not be a problem. When you expect a Boolean value, but you got the string "true", or maybe a null value, you might be tempted to treat them respectively a Boolean `true` and `false`. But what if that function returns a "1", or maybe an object?

In that case you cannot continue and you should return an `UnexpectedValueException`.

This is a snippet from a class that sends and receives data from an HTTP API.

```
function getResultFromHTTP($url) {
    $response = $this->send($url);
    if (! $response || $response->getStatus() >= 400) {
        // An error occurred
        throw new \UnexpectedValueException(
            "No or incorrect result returned");
    }
    return $response->getBody();
}
```

Exceptions

Chapter 7

Miscellaneous Functionality

The SPL is not only a library of iterators, interfaces and data structures. There is plenty of other functionality available in the SPL that can help with your daily work. Since they are not part of any of the above classes, they are provided as "miscellaneous" functionality inside the SPL.

Miscellaneous Functions

Below is a list of miscellaneous functions.

class_implements()

`class_implements()` is a generic function to return ALL the interfaces that the current object has implemented. It will return the interfaces in order of implementation, so the last entry is the earliest interface implemented by either itself or a parent class.

You can either feed it an object, or a string with a class name. The second argument can let you prevent automatic loading of the class, which means the function will fail when the class is not already loaded. There are probably good reasons for this argument, but I haven't found them yet.

You should be aware that when you want to check for a specific interface, that you should use "instanceof" operator instead of this class_implements(). It will not only be faster, but also easier for you to implement:

```
if (!$iterator instanceof Countable) {
    print "This iterator's elements are not Countable";
}
```

versus the class_implements() function:

```
$interfaces = class_implements($iterator);
if (! in_array("Countable", $interfaces) ) {
    print "This iterator's elements are not Countable";
}
```

class_parents()

class_parents() will return the parent classes of an object. It will return all the classes in order so the last entry is the earliest extended class. Just like the class_implements() and class_uses(), you can either give it an object or a string with a class name.

The following example:

```
print_r(class_parents("RecursiveDirectoryIterator"));
```

will return (on next page)

```
Array
(
    [FilesystemIterator] => FilesystemIterator
    [DirectoryIterator] => DirectoryIterator
    [SplFileInfo] => SplFileInfo
)
```

Miscellaneous Functionality

class_uses()

This function will return the traits (introduced in PHP 5.4) of a specific class. class_uses() works the same way as the class_implements() and class_parents() functions, but with one big exception: it will only return traits defined by the class, but not from any parent classes. This is because information about parent traits is not directly available inside a class.

iterator_apply()

This function is somewhat similar to the array_walk() function, but it works on iterators instead of arrays. To be more precise, it works on anything that has the Traversable interface implemented so classes that implement IteratorAggregates will also work with this function. You need to pass a callback function and additional arguments to the function that will be called on each item that will be iterated.

```
function print_caps(Iterator $iterator) {
    echo strtoupper($iterator->current()) . PHP_EOL;
    return true;
}

$it = new ArrayIterator(
    array("Apples", "Bananas", "Cherries"));
iterator_apply($it, "print_caps", array($it));
```

Be aware that your callback function does not receive any arguments unless you have supplied them through the iterator_apply(). Most of the time, the array($it) would be enough since it would supply the callback function of the actual iterator so you can use the standard current() and key() methods of the iterator.

Also note that your callback must supply a value that evaluates to Boolean true (returning "true" is in fact, the easiest way to do this). If you would return false, iterator_apply would stop with the iterations. The iterator would not be reset, so it will point to the last item that was processed by the iterator_apply.

```
$it = new ArrayIterator(
array("one", "two", "three", "four", "five"));
iterator_apply($it, "cb", array($it));
print "After iterator_apply: " . $it->current() . PHP_EOL;
exit;
function cb(Traversable $it) {
    print "Current is now: " . $it->current() . PHP_EOL;
    if ($it->current() == "three") {
        return false;
    }
    return true;
}
```

iterator_count()

Internally, the `iterator_count()` function is implemented as an `iterator_apply()` function with a simple callback function that increases a variable. That variable is returned by `iterator_count()`.

Suppose you have a database result set iterator (sometimes called a cursor). It contains the records returned, but they are not loaded until they are actually needed by the `current()` method. So when you are going to count the number of records in your result set, it would do so by loading every record instead of returning some metadata through it's `count()` function. So be careful when using this function for counting elements. It might become a performance bottleneck in your application.

iterator_to_array()

On occasion it's useful to create an array from an iterator. This could happen when you need to feed your iterator elements to a function that does not understand iterators.

It generates an array by collecting all the elements. With the `$use_keys` argument, you can decide whether or not your array should contains the matching keys as well.

spl_classes()

This function is in the same family as the `phpversion()`, `phpinfo()`

Miscellaneous Functionality

and `phpcredits()` functions. It will return an array of all functions and classes defined by the SPL. Note that there are better ways of finding out whether or not certain SPL functionality exists and so this function doesn't really serve a real purpose. The list that is generated from this function is actually a hardcoded list. Due to bugs, it may be (although not very likely) that functionality exists that is not available in this list, or worse, the list returns functionality that in fact isn't there anymore. A good example is the `GlobIterator` that might not be available on all systems, but will always be present inside this list.

Be advised that when you use this function to check for SPL functionality you always should make sure it's really present by using the `class_exists()` and `function_exists()`.

spl_object_hash()

This function returns a hash for a specific object. This hash is a 32-char long hexadecimal number which is created by fetching a global 32bit random number and XOR'ing this number with the handle and handlers of the current object. It's a very fast way of generating a hash which can be used for comparing objects but it has some drawbacks you have to consider:

- Because `spl_object_hash` creates hashes based on a random number, every time a new PHP process starts, the SAME object will have a different number. Therefore, you cannot store the `spl_object_hash`, and use it to compare the same object later on another page request done by the user.

- Because of point one, storing an object with `serialize()` to a file, and unserializing it inside another process, will result in another hash.

- When the object is freed, another object can re-use that same handle. Therefore it is possible that two different objects (even though one is already freed from memory), can result in `spl_object_hash()` returning the same object.

- You cannot use `spl_object_hash` to compare objects since changing a property on an object will not change its `spl_object_hash` output.

```
class Bar {
}
// Create 2 bar objects
$bar1 = new Bar();
$bar2 = new Bar();
// Will have 2 different hashes
print spl_object_hash($bar1) . PHP_EOL;
print spl_object_hash($bar2) . PHP_EOL;
// Unset bar2, and directly create a bar3
unset($bar2);
$bar3 = new Bar();
// bar3 will (probably) reuse the "hash" of bar2
print spl_object_hash($bar3) . PHP_EOL;
```

SPL Autoloading

In many languages, it's common practice, or sometimes even necessary, that you provide one class per file. This increases readability and performance in case you need to use only one class in a file that would contain ten.

However, one of the drawbacks is that every time we need to use a class, we need to include the filename of that class first, otherwise PHP doesn't know about that class which results in an error. With the help of autoloading we can automatically include source files when classes are instantiated that do not exist. Whenever this happens, PHP will call the magic global `function __autoload()`, with the class as an argument. It is up to you to provide a function that automatically includes the file that contains that class.

Most people call the SPL autoloader an autoloader stack. This is not correct since it is based on FIFO (first-in first-out), just like a queue. In other words, the SPL autoloader is a queue, not a stack.

But since the arrival of frameworks and big components that many people nowadays include in their application, there still can be only one `__autoload()` function inside your application. But most frameworks provide their own autoload functionality. This means that if you want to use that framework, you have to copy that "autoloader" code into your own `__autoload()` function or link to the autoloading function from your own autoloader. But handling autoloading this way is very error-prone and not really scalable.

The SPL has introduced functionality for dealing with autoloading in a better way. Instead of having one global `__autoload()` function, you can use multiple autoloaders. This way you can start with your own autoloader function while the frameworks and components you include will use their own autoloaders.

spl_autoload_call()

This function "forces" PHP to load the requested class through the autoloader. It's not really a very useful function though since this is done automatically whenever a class is not found by PHP.

spl_autoload_extensions()

This function will return or optionally set the file extensions which the `spl_autoload()` function will look for. It isn't used when you implement your own autoloader functionality, but you can use them if you want.

> When adding your own extensions, make sure you include the '.', and make sure you don't leave any spaces between extensions. For instance ".php,.class,.inc.php" is correct, but "php, class, inc.php" is not.

spl_autoload_functions()

This will return an array of registered autoload functions. If there are no autoloaders registered through `spl_autoload_register()`, but there is an (old-style) `__autoload()` function available, that one will be returned. If there is no `__autoload()` present and no SPL autoloaders are registered, it will return a Boolean `false`.

Miscellaneous Functionality

spl_autoload_register()

This function will add a new autoloader function in the autoloading queue. When a class needs to be auto-loaded, PHP will call every function in this queue. After every autoloader call it will check whether or not the needed class is loaded. If not, it will load the next autoloader in the queue until the end of the queue has reached. This would imply that you would register the autoloaders that will load the most classes as early as possible in the queue (you can prepend the autoloaders if needed).

If you call this method with an already registered callback, it will not be added again to the list.

Note that this function will "overwrite" the global `__autoload()` function: you either use the SPL_autoload_register or the `__autoload()` function. You cannot use them both. If you still want to use the `__autoload()` function as well, you can add it with `spl_autoload_register()`.

When the `$throw` argument is set to true, it will throw an exception whenever the autoloader could not be added to the autoload queue. This can happen when the callback is not callable or does not exist.

> You cannot register the spl_autoload_call() function itself. This will throw a LogicException.

The `$prepend` argument makes it possible to add the function to the beginning of the queue instead of at the end. This can be useful when you have an autoloader that will find files most of the time. By adding it in front of the queue it will be served as first which will speed up autoloading. Note however, that others can also call `spl_autoload_register()` with the `$prepend = true` value, those functions will then be placed in front of yours so you can never know for sure your that function will be exactly the first (it's possible to figure this out with the `spl_autoload_function()` call so you can warn the user, but doing so would probably take more time than you would gain).

spl_autoload_unregister()

This will remove a function from the autoloading queue. Note that when you remove the last function, it does not mean that the standard __autoload function will be called again. Once this has been replaced by the first `spl_autoload_register()` call, it will not be activated anymore. You can however, make sure it's activated by calling:
`spl_autoload_register("__autoload");`

spl_autoload()

This function is the default autoloader function from the SPL. If you don't register your own autoloader, but call the `spl_autoload_register()` without a callback function, it will automatically register the `spl_autoload()` method. Note that this will only work when it is the FIRST call to `spl_autoload_register()`. It doesn't even work when you register and unregister another function first.

When you unregister the function "spl_autoload_call", it will remove ALL autoloaders from the queue. This is a special condition inside the PHP core that may or may not be removed in the future.

PSR-0 and the SplClassLoader

To ensure framework interoperability, a group of PHP developers and users founded the PHP Standards Requirements Group. This group defines generic ways of dealing with common problems many frameworks must deal with in order to make it easier to use multiple frameworks at the same time.

Presently they have created and accepted a common way for autoloading classes which is described in the PSR-0 specification. It basically defines the way classes are named, and how these classes are mapped to files on disk (for instance, the class `Vendor_Package_Class` would reside in the directory `Vendor/Package/Class.php`) and how to deal with namespacing, etc.

Miscellaneous Functionality

The accepted PSR-0 standard can be found at:

https://github.com/php-fig/fig-standards/blob/master/accepted/PSR-0.md

The `SplClassLoader` is a function that would simplify the way PHP files are loaded. This class would be able to autoload any class from a framework or library that is PSR-0-compliant. This not only makes it easier (and a bit faster, although marginally) for autoloading classes, but it also means that it makes it much easier to incorporate frameworks and libraries into your own code.

At the time of writing, the `SplClassLoader` is still in its voting process so there is no official word on whether or not it will be implemented. However, the yeah-votes are in front by a small margin. Depending on how the vote will go, it may be added to the SPL in one of the next releases.

But whether or not the class loader is accepted, following the PSR-0 can be considered as best practice to ensure maximal interoperability between your code and others, now and in the future.

ArrayObject

The `ArrayObject` is the object-oriented equivalent of a standard PHP array. It's not the same as implementing the `ArrayAccess` interface, since that interface only enables the fact you can use `[]` indexing. The `ArrayObject` goes a step further: it consists of array sorting functionality and because the class also implements `Countable`, it allows you to count items directly just like `count($array)` would. Extending this object saves time over creating your own array-object by implementing `Countable`, `ArrayAccess`, etc., since all this

> The ArrayObject uses the STD_PROP_LIST and ARRAY_AS_PROPS flags in the same way as the ArrayIterator. For more information about how these flags work, please take a look at the ArrayIterator in the "Iterator" chapter.

work has been done for you by the `ArrayObject`.

In essence, the `ArrayObject` is remarkably similar to an `ArrayIterator`. In fact, much of the internal code is shared between this class and the `ArrayIterator`. Since the `ArrayObject` by itself is an `IteratorAggregate`, it does not directly implement methods like `current()`, `next()`, `key()`, etc...

Objects vs. Arrays

So the whole point of the `ArrayObject` is to mimic the behavior of an array. So why not use arrays in the first place? The answer lies a bit deeper into the core of PHP.

Normally, when a variable is copied, PHP doesn't really do a copy at all. It merely lets two variables point to the same bit of information. When one of either variable does modifications, then it will duplicate the data, and modify it. From that point on, the two variables are living truly separately. This is known as copy-on-write.

However, it doesn't work the same way for objects. When you create an object, and assign another variable to it (like: `$a = new stdClass(); $b = $a);`), both `$a` and `$b` will always point to the same object. When you modify `$b`, it will be visible in `$a` as well. This is why you should do a "`$b = clone $a;`" if you want to create two separate classes.

This means that an `ArrayObject` acts like an array, but does not suffer from copy-on-write. You don't need to pass it by reference (with the ugly &), and it also means that when modifying the `ArrayObject` in one place, its modification will automatically be visible everywhere.

```
// Copy on write
$a = array("foo", "bar");
$b = $a;
$b[] = "baz";
print_r ($a);     // foo, bar
print_r ($b);     // foo, bar, baz
// Object pass by reference
$a = new ArrayObject();
$a[] = "foo";
$a[] = "bar";
$b = $a;
$b[] = "baz";
print_r (iterator_to_array($a));     // foo, bar, baz
print_r (iterator_to_array($b));     // foo, bar, baz
```

array ArrayObject::exchangeArray (mixed $input)

This exchanges the data from the object to another set of data.

void ArrayObject::setIteratorClass (string $iterator_class)

Since this class extends the `IteratorAggregate`, it needs to have the abstract class `getIterator()` implemented. This method is called when traversing the `ArrayObject` during a `foreach()` loop. However, it might be feasible that you want to define what kind of iterator it should return. The `setIteratorClass()` method sets the class-name of the class that would be defined.

The following code mimics the way this works internally in the `ArrayObject`:

```
class ArrayObject {
    protected $iteratorClassName = "ArrayIterator";
    function getIteratorClass() {
        return  $this->iteratorClassName;
    }
    function setIteratorClass($className) {
        $this->iteratorClassName = $className;
    }
    function getIterator() {
        $class = $this->iteratorClassName
        return $class($this->_array);
    }
}
```

Miscellaneous Functionality

Example

```
$tmp = array("a" => "b", "c" => "d");
$a = new ArrayObject();
$a->setFlags(ArrayObject::ARRAY_AS_PROPS);
$a['foo'] = "bar";
$a['baz'] = "qux";
print_r ($a);
$a->exchangeArray($tmp);
print_r ($a);
```

SPL File handling

The SPL defines a set of objects for handling files and directories.
Not only do they provide most file functionality, but they also are
used by iterators that deal with file and directory traversing. See the
`DirectoryIterator`, `FileSystemIterator` and `GlobIterator`
for more info.

SplFileInfo

This SPL class offers functionality
for retrieving file information. You
construct this class by supplying a
filename, (which doesn't have to exist).
Most of these functions are equivalent
to the standard PHP functionalities, so
`$obj->getAtime()` would be the
equivalent of `fileatime($obj);`

> Many, if not most of these methods will return a RunTimeException when you are accessing information on non-existing files.

public string SplFileInfo::getLinkTarget (void)

This method returns the target of the link. When the file itself is not a link,
it will throw a `RuntimeException`.

public string SplFileInfo::getType (void)

This method is the equivalent of `filetype()` and returns the type of the file. Its type can be one of the following strings: fifo, char, dir, block, file, or socket. When the type of a file is unknown it will throw an E_NOTICE error, and returns the string "unknown".

public void SplFileInfo::setFileClass ([string $class_name])

This method is used to set the class which is used to create objects by the openFile(). Normally, openFile() will return an object of the SplFileObject type, but sometimes you want your own class instead: for instance, when you don't want to treat the file as a text-file, but another type of file.

> You can only set class-names that are based on the SplFileInfo class.

```
class PNGFileObject extends SplFileObject {
    // Methods to read PNG files
}
$tmp = new SplFileInfo("image.png");
$tmp->setFileClass("PNGFileObject");
$foo = $tmp->openFile("r");
// $foo is now a PNGFileObject
```

public void SplFileInfo::setInfoClass ([string $class_name])

Just like the setFileClass() method, the setInfoClass() method decides what kind of objects the getPathInfo() and getFileInfo() methods return. By default they will return SplFileInfo objects.

SplFileObject

This class extends the SplFileInfo class so you can directly use this class to find out its file information, but this class also defines functionality to deal with standard file I/O. It also implements Seekable and RecursiveIterator so that you can seek directly to a specified line inside the file.

This class not only provides all kinds of functionality for reading and writing to text files, but you can also iterate over the file itself. This example mimics the Unix "head" command.

Miscellaneous Functionality

```
// Display the first 10 lines from /my/file.txt
$file = new SplFileObject("/my/file.text");
$it = new LimitIterator($file, 0, 10);
foreach ($it as $line) {
   print $line;
}
```

Even though this class implements the `RecursiveIterator`, the `hasChildren()` and `getChildren()` methods always will return false.

public void setMaxLineLen (int $max_len)

When reading lines, PHP will read characters until this value is reached or when a newline is detected. When `$max_len` is less than zero it will throw a `DomainException`. When `$max_len` is set to zero, it will read the complete line regardless of size.

public string SplFileObject::fgetss ([string $allowable_tags])

Reads a line from the file and automatically strips HTML tags, or the tags not inside the `$allowable_tags` list. Note when you don't specify a maximum line length with the `SetMaxLineLen()` method, or when you set the maximum line length to 0, this method will only read the first 1024 bytes from the line.

Note that SplFileObject is only useful for text files. Binary files cannot be correctly parsed by SplFileObject.

public void setFlags (int $flags)

There are different modes in which `SplFileObject` can read/write file lines. With this method you can set/unset these modes. All modes are binary so it's possible to set flags using, for instance: `DROP_NEW_LINE | SKIP_EMPTY`

- `DROP_NEW_LINE` - Strips away the line endings.

- `READ_AHEAD` - Already reads the next line when the iterator calls the `rewind()` or `next()` methods.

Miscellaneous Functionality

- SKIP_EMPTY - Skip empty lines. Note that the keys returned by the iterator will always be sequential. This means that the key numbering does not have to correspond with the line numbering!

- READ_CSV - This will read every line as a CSV (character separated value) line. Instead of the actual line, the current() will return an array with all fields. The CSV parser also correctly reads multi lined CSV values. You can use the setCSVControl() method to decide which characters to use for delimiting, enclosing and escaping your CSV file.

Example

Here is a simple example that takes the current file and reverses all the lines into another file.

```
$src = new SplFileObject(__FILE__, "r");
$dst = new SplFileObject("/tmp/newfile.txt", "w");
foreach ($src as $line) {
    $line = strrev($line);
    $dst->fwrite($line);
}
```

SplTempFileObject

The SplTempFileObject is almost identical to the SplFileObject so almost all of its functionality is the same. The only thing that is different is the way files are created during constructing. Normally, they are directly written to disk but in this case it depends on the $max_memory value you give during construction of the object.

Use this class when you need to work with temporary files that may or may not be written to disk. After closing the file, it will be automatically deleted from disk or erased from memory.

SplTempFileObject::__construct([int max_memory])

The max_memory argument decides where and how the file is stored:

- A positive value will store the file in memory until it's larger than this value. At that point the temporary file is written to disk.

- A max_memory of zero will directly write a temporary file to disk.

- A negative value will store the file in memory only.

- When no max_memory is given it will default to a value of 2MB.

    The implementation of temporary files is done with the `php:_memory` and the `php:_temp(/maxmemory:N)` streams.

Miscellaneous Functionality

10255509R00104

Printed in Great Britain
by Amazon.co.uk, Ltd.,
Marston Gate.